LIES
MY PREACHER
TOLD ME

LIES
MY PREACHER
TOLD ME

AN HONEST LOOK AT THE OLD TESTAMENT

BRENT A. STRAWN

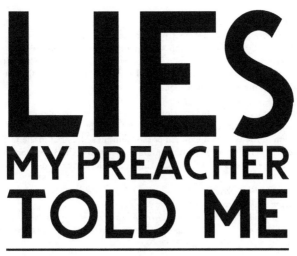

WESTMINSTER
JOHN KNOX PRESS
LOUISVILLE • KENTUCKY

First edition
Published by Westminster John Knox Press
Louisville, Kentucky

21 22 23 24 25 26 27 28 29 30—10 9 8 7 6 5 4 3 2 1

Book design by Drew Stevens
Cover design by designpointinc.com
Cover illustration: The Fall, *after 1479 (oil on panel) (detail of 13000), Hugo van der Goes (c.1440–1482) / Kunsthistorisches Museum, Vienna, Austria /* © *Gordon Roberton Photography Archive / Bridgeman Images*

Library of Congress Cataloging-in-Publication Data

Names: Strawn, Brent A., author.
Title: Lies my preacher told me : an honest look at the Old Testament / Brent A. Strawn.
Description: Louisville, Kentucky : Westminster John Knox Press, 2021. | Includes bibliographical references. | Summary: "This concise volume addresses ten common "lies" or mistruths about the Old Testament, explaining why stories and laws written thousands of years ago, centuries before Christ, are enriching and indispensable for modern Christians. Written by a leading scholar in Old Testament and designed for easy reading and group discussion, this book will expand your thinking about the Old Testament"-- Provided by publisher.
Identifiers: LCCN 2020045342 (print) | LCCN 2020045343 (ebook) | ISBN 9780664265717 (paperback) | ISBN 9781646980109 (ebook)
Subjects: LCSH: Bible. Old Testament--Criticism, interpretation, etc.
Classification: LCC BS511.3 .S785 2021 (print) | LCC BS511.3 (ebook) | DDC 221--dc23
LC record available at https://lccn.loc.gov/2020045342
LC ebook record available at https://lccn.loc.gov/2020045343

Most Westminster John Knox Press books are available at special quantity discounts when purchased in bulk by corporations, organizations, and special-interest groups. For more information, please email SpecialSales@wjkbooks.com.

With thanks for faithful Sunday School teachers:

Catherine Novinger†

Debby Russell

David L. Strawn

Michael Mears Bruner

CONTENTS

PREFACE

A word about the title of this book is in order. I admit that at one point I entertained a different title: *Lies My Sunday School Teacher Told Me*. Either version, that one or the current one that blames the dishonesty in question on *preachers*, unabashedly borrows from the well-known book by James W. Loewen, *Lies My Teacher Told Me: Everything Your American History Textbook Got Wrong*.[1] I seriously doubt that the present volume will, like Loewen's, sell "nearly 2 million copies" as the cover of his revised edition states, but hope springs eternal!

The title isn't the only way the current book echoes Loewen's. He makes sure to point out that his book never itself "bashes teachers."[2] Similarly, I certainly do not mean by my title any disrespect to preachers or Sunday school teachers—well, not the good ones anyway. There are a lot of very good examples of preachers and teachers out there in the real world and everyone knows that the church desperately needs a lot more of both. That said, no one is above making mistakes in the pulpit or in the lectern (or in the pews, which is the end point of all that preaching and teaching); I am confident that I've made countless ones myself. These mistakes aren't always malicious—let's hope not, at any rate. Instead, the mistruths that are propagated in so many churches are mostly the sad result of people — preachers or teachers, ordained people or lay folk — being ill-informed or at least not fully informed.[3] The Bible is a big book, after all; big *and* complex. It is easy for people to make a few mistakes (present company included) when the subject matter is that large and complicated, not to mention that significant. We are, after all, talking about *Holy Scripture* here. But wherever they come from, and however the situation has come to pass, this book is about ten things that many people erroneously believe about the largest and most difficult part of Holy Scripture: the Old Testament. I hope that, as little as it is, this book might nevertheless begin to set the record straight on these matters so that others are not similarly misled.

I am thankful to the good people at Westminster John Knox, especially Jessica Miller Kelley for proposing this volume and her hugely helpful editing, for their patience while I worked on it amidst other projects, and for their excellent work in getting it to press despite the various problems I caused along the way. I'm also thankful to friends and family who listened to my ideas about the book, discussed it with me, and/or submitted their own mistruths, which were often better than the ones on my original list. I specifically want to mention Jon Stallsmith, Collin Cornell, Ryan Bonfiglio, Justin Pannkuk, Reese and Beverly Verner, and my four best teachers: my wife, Holly, and our three children, Caleb, Annie, and Micah.

Speaking of quartets of good teachers, I dedicate this volume to four faithful Sunday school teachers, especially because the book is designed for use in educational contexts in churches. Catherine Novinger, now among God's saints in light, is the earliest Sunday school teacher I can remember. It was in her class, while still a preteen, that I first felt a call to ministry, which I suspect was facilitated in some fashion by her regular insistence that the boys and girls under her tutelage sing "Trust and Obey" every single Sunday morning in a tiny upstairs room at the University Avenue Church of the Nazarene (now Mid-City Church of the Nazarene) in San Diego, California. Debby Russell taught me not long thereafter, in the same room as I recall, while I was still in elementary school. What I remember to this day is how earnestly she cared about what I, young as I was, thought about the Bible lessons. It seems to me that teachers and preachers who take their students and listeners (and their subject matter) with utmost seriousness are, sadly, in shorter supply than we might think. My dad, David Strawn, has always stood out as bucking that trend. He is easily among the most diligent and conscientious of Sunday school teachers I've ever seen (may his tribe increase), devoting hours each week to prepare his lessons (he still does). It showed (it still does). Last but not least, Michael Mears Bruner is a dear friend from my seminary days. We co-taught a Sunday school class on heresies, ancient and modern, at Hopewell Presbyterian Church in Hopewell, New Jersey, more than twenty years ago, and the class remains one of my favorite teaching experiences ever. I learned much from Mears at that time, and that situation has continued ever since, across the miles, whenever we have had the occasion to see each other, simply because he is an unbelievably gifted church teacher (and five times smarter than me, at least, but the latest calculations are revising that figure upward). I am indebted to these four teachers and, no doubt, to many others that I have left unmentioned. In my opinion, all of them are part of that great cloud of witnesses, the communion of saints. As Mark Twain supposedly quipped about believing in infant baptism: "I don't just *believe* in that cloud and communion, I've *seen* it!"

bas
Durham, NC
Spring 2020

LIES *SOMEBODY* TOLD US ABOUT THE OLD TESTAMENT

As noted in the Preface (please take a moment to read it if you haven't already), the title of the present book cribs from a well-known book by James W. Loewen: *Lies My Teacher Told Me*, which is subtitled *Everything Your American History Textbook Got Wrong*.[1] Apparently I'm not the only person to take inspiration from Loewen's eye-grabbing title. There are books called *Lies My Doctor Told Me* and even *Lies My Pastor Told Me*.[2] My own title is somewhat tongue in cheek—after all, the situation may not be as sinister as *lying*. Lying implies intentional misrepresentation of the truth, and I suspect—or at least I dearly hope—that that is rarely the case in church contexts. Instead, the situation is usually far more innocent than that. For various reasons, people often feel compelled to speak about all sorts of matters without really knowing what they are talking about, and, when they do so, the result can become a laissez-faire attitude toward the truth. That isn't lying per se, but it is no less damaging. Harry G. Frankfurt, a moral philosopher who taught at Princeton University for years, has argued (quite seriously but also somewhat tongue in cheek) that people who don't really care about truth are actually a greater threat than liars. Liars know the truth, Frankfurt says, they just misrepresent it on purpose. But people who don't care about the truth . . . well, *they just don't care*.[3] Truth doesn't matter to them; maybe it doesn't even exist for them.

Given my hope that things weren't quite yet malicious, I decided to call each of the topics I discuss in this book "mistruths" rather than bald-faced lies. Even so, as Frankfurt suggests, the end result of a mistruth could be just as, if not more damaging than, a lie. In the case of a lie, the truth simply needs to be brought to light for things to be set right. That is easier said than done, of course. As Loewen notes in his own work on lies in history textbooks and in history classrooms, there is often no shortage of factual evidence, but there is also no shortcut in the time-consuming tasks of amassing and assessing that evidence.[4] Mistruths are like misinformation in this way: they are hard to expose so as to set the record straight. Mistruths are thus far more insidious and intractable than a bald-faced lie: they extend their tendrils to all sorts of areas, like the roots of a tree, so that uprooting them is often very difficult. Even if you chop one down to size, the stump is likely to sprout again. Surely the Internet, especially social media, is the fastest fertilizer known to humankind to facilitate such regrowth.

Given these various considerations, I have no doubt that not every reader will agree with my assessment of some of these mistruths—that is to be expected. I only ask readers to keep open minds and to keep searching for the truth, the whole truth, so help them God—the truth about God's Word. Contrary to what some Christians have been led to believe, erroneously, that Word is also found in the Old Testament. That comment leads directly to the first mistruth.

THE OLD TESTAMENT IS "SOMEONE ELSE'S MAIL"

In my first few years as a seminary professor, I frequently commuted to work with a friend, let's call him Tom, who was on staff at the same institution. We had a number of things in common but there were also differences that became apparent fairly early on—the respective cleanliness of our vehicles comes to mind, though I won't reveal whose was cleaner (okay, it was mine). At some point in one of our commutes, another difference rose to particular clarity when Tom expressed a bit of confusion as to why I cared so much for the Old Testament (my academic specialty).

"That's *somebody else's* mail!" he said, appearing a bit flabbergasted if not angry, after I tried to explain why I studied the Old Testament and thought it so important, equally important (I probably remarked) as the New Testament.

I can't remember what I said after Tom's comment. I admit that it caught me off guard, so I probably didn't say much, if anything. Evidently Tom's statement was sufficiently disturbing to me that it encoded in my long-term memory so that I remember it to this day. Whatever the case, I know what I would say now, if I could rewind the conversation and do it all over again. Here's how it would go down:

Tom: "That's *somebody else's* mail!"

Me: "So, you live in Corinth, Tom?"

Now there are plenty of Corinths peppered across the United States of America, but I mean by this witty and far too-late retort the ancient Greek city to which Paul wrote a couple of famous letters. Tom most certainly did *not* live in *that* Corinth. But for some odd reason Tom thought that the Old Testament was "somebody else's mail," while at the same time imagining that First and Second Corinthians were letters somehow addressed *to him*. But, of course, they weren't. And yet, in a way, they are! Both points deserve some discussion.

1. On one hand, 1 and 2 Corinthians were definitely *not* addressed to Tom — not originally — because the Epistles to the Corinthians, no less than other letters of Paul or other writings in the New Testament, were written to a group of Christians in a drastically different context and situation than the state that Tom and I were living in at the time (Kentucky, ca. 1998). So, no: we weren't living in ancient Corinth and the letters to the Corinthians in the *New* Testament are clearly and obviously "someone else's mail." Not only is this true, most Christians today would not want to be members of that ancient church in Corinth. You think your church has problems! Corinth was *worse*: they had more than their fair share of dissension, sexual scandal, problems with worship, and so on and so forth. Well . . . come to think about it, that list makes it sound like many people today *do* belong to churches like the one in ancient Corinth!

2. While nothing to celebrate, that last point shows how in another, very real sense the letters to the Corinthians *are* addressed to Tom (and me) because they are letters written *to Christians*. "To God's church that is in Corinth," is how Paul puts it (1 Cor 1:2; 2 Cor 1:1 CEB). Since those

ancient Corinthians were followers of Christ, and Tom and I are too, we can somehow receive Paul's words across the miles and millennia and hear them as our own.

Now I suspect that part of what Tom meant in his remark is that, in contrast to the New Testament, the books of the Old Testament weren't originally written *for or to Christians* in the same way that the Corinthian correspondence was. That is true to a degree, but the first point mentioned above indicates that the Corinthian correspondence was also *not* written directly to Tom. How then did Tom come to see it and receive it as his "own" mail?

Simple: Because 1 and 2 Corinthians are now part of Holy Scripture.

The inclusion of the Epistles of Paul (and the rest of the New Testament writings) in a corpus of literature that the church deems to be a special, even sacred collection — the technical term is "canon" — transports letters that were originally meant for a very different (and cantankerous) group of Christians way back when, and places them front and center, here and now, as letters also for Christians today, even if we don't live in Corinth, Mississippi, let alone Corinth, Greece, and despite the fact that we live in the *twenty*-first, not the first, century after Christ. (It goes without saying that we may be equally cantankerous as the folks back then.)

So, no, the letters to the Corinthians were *not* addressed to Tom. They, too, are "someone else's mail." But, yes, on the other hand, these letters *are* addressed to Tom because they are now part of Christian Scripture.

But here's the most important part — the truth to correct Mistruth 1 — *the same is true for the Old Testament*. Sure, the Old Testament wasn't originally written to Christian believers in the twenty-first century, but neither was the New Testament. But the Old Testament, no less than the New, is now part of the canon of Christian Scripture. That means that the Old Testament, not unlike the New, and in fact, *exactly* like the New, is now *our* mail. It is no different in this regard than the letters to the Corinthians, let alone those letters of Paul written to specific, named individuals who are not named "Tom" (or "Brent" for that matter): Timothy, Titus, Philemon. The letters that are addressed to particular individuals would seem by definition, or rather by addressee, the ultimate instance of "not my mail."

How did the Old Testament come to be included in Christian Scripture such that it, too, is our mail? That is a big question that cannot be answered fully here. A few brief remarks must suffice for now.

To begin with, the earliest Christian community was made up entirely of Jews, which means that Holy Scripture was, prior to the rise of the early Jewish Christian community, for all intents and purposes, the Old Testament and the Old Testament alone.[1] The Old Testament was, therefore, *the only Scripture* that early (Jewish) Christians knew. Or that Jesus knew. When the New Testament writers speak of Scripture, therefore—say, in the famous verse in 2 Timothy 3:16, which states that "all scripture is inspired by God and is useful for teaching"—they are referring to the Old Testament.[2] This is, in fact, why the Old Testament features so prominently throughout the New Testament—in both explicit ways and in ways that lurk under the surface at the level of allusion and echo.

The explicit ways are how the Old Testament is frequently cited in the New Testament: for example, the many times Matthew writes that this or that thing in his Gospel happened in order to fulfill what had been written in the Old Testament (Matt. 1:22; 2:15, 23; 4:14; 8:17; 12:17; 13:35; 21:4). Old Testament citations in the New Testament run in the hundreds. Less obvious, especially in English translation, but even more prevalent are the "under the surface" echoes and allusions to the Old Testament found throughout the New Testament. These number in the *thousands*. One way to put this would be to say that if you tried to remove all of the Old Testament "stuff" from the body of the New Testament, the patient wouldn't survive the surgery.

Even after the early church opened up to Gentiles, Paul continued to evangelize in the synagogues in addition to his work with non-Jewish populations. And it is this very same Paul—the one Tom thought was speaking directly to him—who *constantly* depended on the Old Testament to make his arguments about faith, the meaning of Jesus, and so on and so forth: to both Jews and Gentiles. Paul, that is, read the Old Testament as *his own mail* not just when he was a Pharisee but even, and this is a very important point, *after* his "conversion" to Christ on the road to Damascus.

In one of his most famous letters, Romans, Paul explains how Gentile Christians have been grafted into the tree that is Israel (11:11–24). In this very important image, in this very important part of this very important letter, Gentile Christianity isn't something altogether new, nor independent, but, instead, simply a branch freshly attached to a tree that preexisted it. Branches, especially ones that have been grafted in, take sustenance from the trunk and the root system, which, in Paul's image, are nothing less than the story of Israel and God's work in the Old Testament. So, according to the great Apostle to the Gentiles, now that Christians are part of Israel's family tree, nothing that belongs to that tree is not also ours, even if only belatedly and secondarily. There is nothing, that is, that is not our mail or that is not directed to us who call ourselves Christians simply because we, too, are now part of biblical Israel—thanks to a gifted Gardener who specializes in tree grafts. All of what was said to Israel in the Old Testament is thus said also to Christians, is related to Christians—we who draw life itself, our very sustenance, from that mother tree. That is why Christians have, from day one, consistently looked to the Old Testament for the truth about God and life in the world.

So, contrary to what Tom was misled to believe, the Old Testament is not someone else's mail.[3] It is *our* mail, addressed to us, eminently useful to us — just as 2 Timothy 3:16–17 clearly states:

> Every scripture is inspired by God and is useful for teaching, for showing mistakes, for correcting, and for training character, so that the person who belongs to God can be equipped to do everything that is good. (CEB)

Other texts in the New Testament say the same in hundreds, even thousands of ways, by explicit citation or subtle allusion and echo, but here are two important examples drawn, again, from Paul:

> Whatever was written in the past was written for our instruction so that we could have hope through endurance and through the encouragement of the scriptures. (Rom. 15:4 CEB; see also Rom. 4:23–24)

> These things happened to them [the Israelites] as an example and were written as a warning for us to whom the end of time has come. (1 Cor. 10:11 CEB; see also 1 Cor 9:9–10)

Written *for our instruction*, so *we* could have hope. And also written as a warning *for us*.

It is thus a terrible mistruth to say that the Old Testament is someone else's mail. In fact, this first mistruth may be the most pernicious, most troubling of the ten treated in this little book. That's why it deserves pride (or, perhaps better, shame) of place and must be set right first and foremost, before any and all others. The real truth is that the *entirety* of Scripture—Old Testament and New—is to be viewed and heard as an urgent speaking presence exercising benevolent pressure on our lives.[4] That statement does not mean that the Old Testament (or the New for that matter) is always easy to understand, let alone easy to apply to our lives now. Of course not! It also doesn't mean that the Old Testament is mail to *Christians only*. Of course not! The Old Testament also belongs to Judaism, where it wouldn't be called the "Old Testament" at all but rather something like "Scripture" or "Bible." But these important subjects—interpretation, application, the place of the Old Testament in Christianity *and* in Judaism, along with others—are best taken up with reference to some of the other mistruths treated later (see especially Mistruths 3 and 10). Here, then, instead of Mistruth 1, I offer the following first clarification:

CLARIFICATION 1:
The Old Testament, no less than the New, is Christian Scripture.

QUESTIONS FOR DISCUSSION

1. Have you ever thought the Old Testament was someone else's mail? If so, why? What texts in particular seemed to be not intended for you? If not, why not?
2. Have you ever thought the New Testament was someone else's mail? If so, why? What texts in particular seemed to be not intended for you? If not, why not?
3. Do you find it difficult to think of the Old Testament as "an urgent speaking presence exercising benevolent pressure" on your life? Why or why not?

4. What difference would it make to our reading of Scripture if we thought of all of it, Old Testament and New, as that kind of speaking presence? Would it make a difference in how we think about the Old Testament? The New?
5. Give an example of a time when a biblical text spoke to you directly and you heard it in a way that helped you in some concrete way for the better.

THE OLD TESTAMENT IS A BORING
HISTORY BOOK

There are no doubt several deep-seated reasons that lead people to think the Old Testament is someone else's mail (Mistruth 1), but two seem to loom large. One of them is more theoretical or, better, theological—I take it up next (Mistruth 3). The other is more pragmatic and so, as a result, probably easier to discuss, though it is no less pervasive or powerful. This second reason has to do with how people *experience* the Old Testament, some of which is based on their own first-hand knowledge as readers of it, but some of which is based on perception, even *mis*perception (no surprise) of the Old Testament. In fact, some of that experience seems to be built on little (or no) familiarity with actually reading the Old Testament. It is based on *lack* of experience with the Old Testament as much as experience with it. Whatever the case, this second, more mundane reason for thinking that the Old Testament is someone else's mail, and disliking it to boot, can be captured as Mistruth 2: The Old Testament is a boring history book.

Many years ago, I co-taught a clergy workshop in New Mexico. The topic was how to best preach the Old

Testament. We started with sharing experiences about how or why preaching the Old Testament was especially tricky or difficult. I'll never forget how, as the pastors shared this or that problem or issue, one preacher looked around and solemnly asserted, somewhat authoritatively as I recall:

"People don't like history."

This, evidently, was a reason—whether this preacher's or his flock's—to not preach from the Old Testament or why hearing preaching from the Old Testament proved to be especially difficult in his opinion.

I remember firing back almost immediately:

"And who told you it was a history book?"

My response was probably too quick really, maybe a bit too confrontational. I guess the earlier experience with Tom had paid off: I was locked and loaded for a swift and snarky reply!

There are two parts to Mistruth 2 that need to be unpacked and addressed. The first is that the Old Testament is *boring*, the second is that it is a *history book*. Let's begin with the latter.

On first blush, much of the Old Testament does strike the casual reader as a history book. It starts, after all, "In the beginning" in the first chapter of Genesis with the rest of that book presenting a picture of the early days of human existence, including various genealogies that report who is related to whom and that run right down to the ancestors of the people of Israel: Abraham and Sarah; Isaac and Rebekah; and Jacob, Rachel, Leah, and all their children. After that, we learn how what began as a nuclear family grew into a large group of people, a nation even, and how the people of Israel end up in Egypt where they are enslaved and oppressed, and then how they escape Egypt and eventually arrive at Canaan (Exodus through Deuteronomy).

Then we read about how the Israelites took possession of that land, which was promised to Abraham and his descendants long ago (but only a few pages back), and then learn of the leaders and events who followed the great Moses in that endeavor (Joshua through Ruth). The Bible next tells the story of the last of the judges, who is also the first of the prophets, Samuel, who anoints Saul as the first king of Israel. Saul's reign is a mixed bag at best (1 Samuel), and he is followed by David, who is also something of a mixed bag (see, e.g., 2 Sam. 11), and then by his son Solomon, who is most certainly a mixed bag (see 1 Kgs. 11). By this point we are in the book of Kings where we learn that, after Solomon, the people-turned-nation-turned-kingdom of Israel divides in two, with Israel in the north and Judah in the south, each with its own succession of kings, most of whom were . . . well, decidedly mixed bags — or, more accurately, almost entirely bad with only a few exceptions. Second Kings ends on two low points: with the kingdom of Israel falling to the Assyrian Empire (2 Kgs. 17), and the kingdom of Judah, and its capital city, Jerusalem, falling to the Babylonian Empire about a century and a half, but only eight chapters, later (2 Kgs. 25).

All of that does seem like a decent swath of history, boring or otherwise. After 2 Kings (the twelfth book of thirty-nine in the Protestant ordering, roughly a third of the way in), however, the Bible does *not* read like a history book, boring or otherwise. Chronicles retells a good bit of what has come before, especially material familiar from Samuel and Kings, but it doesn't go much further than where 2 Kings leaves off. After this "refrain," the books of Ezra and Nehemiah give us some account of life during and especially after the destruction and exile of Judah and then after the return to that land following 538 BCE[1] (the time of the edict of the Persian king Cyrus). The book of Esther, which comes next, takes place during Persian rule but doesn't cover a long span of time. So, after 2 Kings 25, we can say that Chronicles, Ezra, Nehemiah, and Esther *sort of* continue a "historical" account, but not smoothly or seamlessly—not, that is, like Exodus through Deuteronomy or Joshua through Kings.

After Esther, all bets are off. The books of Job, Psalms, Proverbs, Ecclesiastes, and the Song of Solomon do not tell Israelite *history*. In fact, they seem mostly unconcerned with any of that, with very few exceptions. After these books come the Prophets, including Daniel and Lamentations, which in English Bibles are mixed in among the three major (Isaiah, Jeremiah, Ezekiel) and the twelve "minor" prophets (Hosea through Malachi). Most of these books are connected in one way or another with points in Israel's history. Lamentations, for instance, is a poetic dirge about the destruction of Jerusalem; the first part of Daniel discusses the hero and his colleagues in the courts of Babylon and Persia; and most of the prophetic books begin with superscriptions that tie the prophet in question to the reigns of specific kings. But what happens in these books is not primarily history-telling like a modern book on American or European history for at least two reasons.

1. The first reason is that history writing in the ancient world was different than it is now. Ancient writers didn't have the same concerns (or standards) with regard to fact-checking that we do, probably because they didn't have the same kind of access to facts like we do. Nowadays, for instance, a history of ancient Israel would have to take the full range of archaeological data into consideration. Back then, archaeology as a discipline didn't exist—there were no carefully controlled excavations of previously inhabited sites. Neither did every biblical author systematically consult all available sources, including accounts of the same events written by other historians—though some evidently did (see Luke 1:1–4). This is not to disparage ancient history writing (or writers), whether inside the Bible or outside it; it is just to say that such an endeavor was very different back then than contemporary history writing is now.

2. The second reason why what is found in the Bible isn't primarily "history" as we conceive it is that the biblical authors thought about history in general very differently than modern historians do. To list only the most obvious difference: modern historians—secular ones at any rate—do not consider God to be a cause in, say, the Great Depression or the Watergate scandal. The biblical authors, in contrast, consider God to be a major, if not the primary, cause in a great host of events recounted in Scripture. The fall of the northern kingdom to Assyria, for instance, is not because of inept foreign policy, poor economic development, or inadequate defense spending. Instead:

> All this happened because the Israelites sinned against the LORD their God, who brought them up from the land of Egypt, out from under the power of Pharaoh, Egypt's king. They worshipped other gods. . . . They did evil things that made the LORD angry. They worshipped images about which the LORD had said, Don't do such things! The LORD warned Israel and Judah through all the prophets and seers, telling them, Turn from your evil ways. Keep my commandments and my regulations in agreement with the entire Instruction that I commanded your ancestors and sent through my servants the prophets. But they wouldn't listen. . . . They deserted all the commandments of the LORD their God. They made themselves two metal idols cast in the shape of calves and made a sacred pole. They bowed down to all the heavenly bodies. They served Baal. They burned their sons and daughters alive. They practiced divination and sought omens. They gave themselves over to doing what was evil in the LORD's eyes and made him angry. So the LORD was very angry at Israel. He removed them from his presence. Only the tribe of Judah was spared. (2 Kgs 17:7, 11b–14a, 16–18 CEB)

According to the biblical authors, *theology*—not economy, politics, foreign relations, or whatever else—is the main thing that moves human history, even when those authors chose to write things that, to our ears, otherwise sound a lot like modern history writing.

Another example of this point is the account of the Israelite king Omri, who reigned from 879–869 BCE. Evidence from outside the Bible, from ancient Near Eastern sources, indicates that Omri was an important king, a major political player, but 1 Kings devotes only six verses to him (1 Kgs. 16:23–28). The author of Kings is ultimately only interested in the question of whether Omri was faithful to God or not—that's all that really mattered. Since Omri wasn't faithful, the author of Kings isn't much interested in him, moving on quickly to the next king and next episode in Israel's drama of infidelity.

Examples like these (and many more could be added) show that the Old Testament is *not* exclusively and not even primarily a history book. There *is* history in the Bible, to be sure, but it is *not* a history book—certainly not a modern one. Instead it is a book about religion, faith, God. To categorize the Bible as a history book is therefore to make a serious category error and to miss its major points. By our modern standards, the Old Testament (and all ancient history writing) falls far short of "pure" history writing. By its own content, the Old Testament is clearly about much, much more than "mere" history. So, to correct the first part of Mistruth 2: no, the Old Testament is not a history book.

But is the Old Testament *boring*? That's the second part of Mistruth 2 that needs to be discussed—and it should be separated from the first, historical part. Boring is, after all, in the eye of the beholder. Contrary to the New Mexico preacher's assertion, some people quite like history (they seem to be a small though distinguished crew). Others, however, find the presentation of the monarchs in the book of Kings boring, with others disliking (to put it mildly) the genealogical lists found in the Bible (including Matt. 1:1–17 and Luke 3:23–38), with yet still others finding the Epistles of Paul downright intolerable. In each of these scenarios, the situation seems to have less to do with the literature in question and more with the reader who reads that literature. Some find this part boring, others find that part boring. Whatever the case, is there a solution to Bible-reading boredom? Yes, according to Ellen F. Davis: it is *knowing what to look for*.[2] If you know what to look for—and even more basically *how* to look, how *to read* (with patience, care, and attention)—it is typically the case that you will find plenty of things to see and wonder about that will keep you occupied and interested, far from boredom. Things like why Omri and so many other kings are given such short shrift. Or why a prostitute and an immigrant show up in the genealogy of Jesus (Matt. 1:5). And so on and so forth. Boredom will soon be a thing of the past!

CLARIFICATION #2:
The Old Testament is about far more (and far less) than history, and it can be endlessly fascinating to those with eyes to see, ears to hear, and patience to read.

QUESTIONS FOR DISCUSSION

1. Have you ever thought of the Old Testament, or the New for that matter, primarily as a history book? Was that good or bad in your perspective?
2. How might some parts of the Bible be "history" or "historical" and other parts not? What problems do you see in either perspective?

3. Does thinking about the Old Testament as something other than history make you want to read it more? Less? Trust it more? Less?
4. What parts of the Old Testament have you found boring? Are these parts explicitly historical? Are they sometimes understood to be history? What parts of the Old Testament do you find exciting? Are these the less or nonhistorical parts?
5. What strategies can you imagine that would help you read the Bible with greater care, patience, and attention?

THE OLD TESTAMENT HAS BEEN RENDERED PERMANENTLY OBSOLETE

This mistruth is a doozy. Whole books—lots of them, in fact—have been written both for and against the Old Testament's obsolescence. I can't hope to do justice to the importance and depth of the subject here.[1] Even so, this mistruth *must* be treated if only because it, along with the question of the Old Testament's boringness (Mistruth 2), helps to explain Mistruth 1: why some people think the Old Testament is "someone else's mail." In fact, in the grand scheme of things, Mistruth 3 may well be the most pervasive of all the mistruths we've been misled to believe about the Old Testament. If Mistruth 3 can get set straight, a lot of other problems with the Old Testament disappear. Since Mistruth 3 is such a big issue—a very large mistake to correct— things that are said in some of the other chapters of this book, even the book as a whole, can be seen as addressing it in one way or another.

Let's begin, though, with why someone might assert that the Old Testament has been rendered permanently obsolete. The answer, of course, is because of things we've heard or been taught—that we've been misled to believe—but those things come from *somewhere*. In this particular case they come, no doubt, from many places — once again, too many to list, but here are a few examples:

- The language of "new covenant" used in texts like Luke 22:20, 1 Corinthians 11:25, and 2 Corinthians 3:6, implies an "old covenant" that is . . . well, *old* and, as a result, not nearly as good. Hebrews 8:13 makes the comparison explicit when it says: "In speaking of 'a new covenant,' he [God] has made the first one obsolete. And what is obsolete and growing old will soon disappear." Could anything be more clear?

- This language of "new covenant" is actually where the term "New Testament" comes from (because of the frequent Latin translation of "covenant" as *testamentum*). The "New" Testament, no less than the "new" covenant, not only implies an older version, it often implies (if not asserts) that the old one is no longer in effect. Look, again, at Hebrews 8:13.

- There are numerous places where the New Testament appears to contrast things found in the Old Testament with something different and presumably better. A famous instance is the so-called "antitheses" found in the Sermon on the Mount. There Jesus says, "You have heard it said . . ." (Matt. 5:21, 27, 31, 33, 38, 43) before contrasting that prior word with, "but I say to you . . ." (Matt. 5:22, 28, 32, 34, 39, 44). Another instance might be Jesus' statement about not putting new wine into old wineskins (Matt. 9:17; Mark 2:22; Luke 5:37–38).

- There are various institutions and practices that were central to the Old Testament that are no longer operative within Christianity. The Temple is an obvious example, as is the practice of making sacrifices of animals, special dietary legislation, and so forth.

These examples are significant and are not isolated. More could be said under each point and additional points added.

The problem, however, is that these points (and any others that might be factored in) tell only part of the story, and certainly not all of it. Consider the following items in light of the previous list:

Old Doesn't Mean Bad

"Old" needn't mean "out of date" or "obsolete" or the like. As for Hebrews, as explicit as it is on this matter, it remains the case that Hebrews is profoundly indebted to the Old Testament throughout. Jesus is a new Melchizedek or a new high priest, but the accent in that kind of presentation is as much on *Melchizedek* or *high priest* as it is on *new*. In the ancient world, after all, newness wasn't equated with "right," "good," or "better"; in fact, the opposite was frequently the case. Heresies were often shunned precisely because they were "new." That which was "old," in the sense of tried and true, was better — best to stick with that. In this light, maybe we should replace the adjective "old" in Old Testament with a term like "ancient" in the best sense of that word: elder, venerable, authoritative.[2]

Beyond Hebrews specifically, Mistruth 1 noted how thoroughly dependent the New Testament is on the Old Testament in terms of citation and allusion. The example that was cited there concerned how the Gospel of Matthew repeatedly states that one thing or another took place "in order to fulfill" what had been written before in the Old Testament (see Matt. 1:22; 2:15, 23; 4:14; 8:17; 12:17; 13:35; 21:4).

New Doesn't Mean Christian

As surprising as it may be to hear, the language and concept of a "new covenant" occurs for the first time *not* in the New Testament, but in the Old! The key passage is Jeremiah 31:31–34:

> The days are surely coming, says the LORD, when I will make a new covenant with the house of Israel and

the house of Judah. It will not be like the covenant that I made with their ancestors when I took them by the hand to bring them out of the land of Egypt — a covenant that they broke, though I was their husband, says the LORD. But this is the covenant that I will make with the house of Israel after those days, says the LORD: I will put my law within them, and I will write it on their hearts; and I will be their God, and they shall be my people. No longer shall they teach one another, or say to each other, "Know the LORD," for they shall all know me, from the least of them to the greatest, says the LORD; for I will forgive their iniquity, and remember their sin no more.

This passage states that God gives "the New Covenant" (even "the New Testament," in light of the Latin *testamentum*) first and foremost *to Israel*, not to Christians after the coming of Christ. In fact, the passage I cited from Hebrews 8:13 follows directly upon a citation of Jeremiah 31:31–34 (see Hebrews 8:8–12). That means that the author of Hebrews depends upon Jeremiah 31 to make his point, but it also means that the author's point — about an old way of relating to God that is passing away — applies *already* to Israel, within the Old Testament, which was exactly Jeremiah's point long before Hebrews was written. And it isn't just Jeremiah's point. It's *God's* point, since God is the one talking about "the New Covenant/Testament" in Jeremiah 31. As for the endurance of that covenant with Israel — its liveliness, not its obsolescence — no less an Apostle than Paul said about that covenant that "the gifts and the calling of God are irrevocable" (Rom. 11:29). Or, to quote Jesus, "salvation is from the Jews" (John 4:22).[3]

Jesus Wasn't Replacing the Old
With regard to New Testament passages that seem to denigrate the Old Testament, things aren't always what they

seem. In the case of the "antitheses," not all of them can be located in the Old Testament exactly—some may be interpretations of some of that material (whether by Jesus or by others at his time) since they aren't direct citations. Or some may be pieces of contemporaneous material that didn't end up in the Bible—the line about hating your enemy is a prime example (Matt. 5:43): that just *isn't* found in the Old Testament. Conversely, the positive injunctions by Jesus are often found in the Old Testament. Note, for example, Matthew 5:39:

> "But I say to you, Do not resist an evildoer. But if anyone strikes you on the right cheek, turn the other also."

A laudable and justly famous verse, to be sure! But now let's compare it to some equally laudable, but far less well-known texts from the Old Testament:

> Proverbs 20:22: "Do not say, 'I will repay evil'; wait for the LORD, and he will help you."
>
> Proverbs 24:29: "Do not say, 'I will do to others as they have done to me; I will pay them back for what they have done.'"
>
> Isaiah 50:6: "I gave my back to those who struck me, and my cheeks to those who pulled out the beard; I did not hide my face from insult and spitting."
>
> Lamentations 3:30: "[It is good] to give one's cheek to the smiter, and be filled with insults."

These verses from the Old Testament suggest that Jesus's various "but I say to you" statements might have continued on with "because I read it in our Scriptures!" (which are, of course, the Old Testament; see Mistruth 1). Still further, in many of these "antitheses" (which, by now, we see isn't a good name for these statements) Jesus isn't really against the prior (Old Testament) statement at all, but heavily in favor of it, which is shown by how his rearticulation frequently makes the imperative even more ethically demanding. Not just avoidance of murder, but also avoidance of anger (Matt. 5:21–26). Not just avoidance of adultery, but also avoidance of lust (Matt. 5:27–30). Jesus isn't doing away with the Old Testament commandments. He's making them *harder*. Maybe that is why, very early in the Sermon on the Mount —prior to the first "antithesis"— Jesus says:

> Do not think that I have come to abolish the law or the prophets; I have come not to abolish but to fulfill. For truly I tell you, until heaven and earth pass away, not one letter, not one stroke of a letter, will pass from the law until all is accomplished. Therefore, whoever breaks one of the least of these commandments, and teaches others to do the same, will be called least in the kingdom of heaven; but whoever does them and teaches them will be called great in the kingdom of heaven. For I tell you, unless your righteousness exceeds that of the scribes and Pharisees, you will never enter the kingdom of heaven. (Matt. 5:17–20)

As for the new wine bit, in Luke's account of that saying, Jesus immediately points out that aged wine tastes better: "And no one after drinking old wine desires new wine, but says, 'The old is good'" (Luke 5:39).

Discontinued, Not Rejected

What about "obsolete" institutions like the temple and sacrifice? Ancient Israel also had to deal with the absence of such things during the Babylonian exile, where the exiles had no access to the Temple in Jerusalem or to the sacrificial system. The same is true for Judaism after the destruction of the Second Temple in 70 CE. But quite apart from the exile (or diaspora), the Old Testament is quite clear—*repeatedly*—that God cannot be limited to the Temple (see 2 Sam. 7:4–7; Ezek. 1–3, 7–10; Isa. 6, 66:1; Ps. 2:4; etc.), that the Temple is no "get out of jail free card" (Jer. 7:1–15), and that sacrifice, too (and not unrelatedly), is not ultimately what matters. As Samuel tells King Saul: "Surely, to obey is better than sacrifice, and to heed than the fat of rams" (1 Sam. 15:22b). The psalmists and the Prophets line up to say the same (see, e.g., Ps. 40:6; 50:7–15, 23; 51:16–17; Isa. 1:11–17; Amos 5:21–24; etc.).

The problem with Mistruth 3, therefore, like so many other cases of misinformation, is that it doesn't tell us the whole truth and nothing but the truth, but only a small little part of it. Mistruth 3 isn't completely wrong in all the details it cites on its behalf, but despite that fact, it is still deadly wrong. Such a careless, undisciplined laissez-faire attitude toward the whole truth is a serious problem—not only to Scripture but to truth itself. As I pointed out in the Introduction, that kind of uncaring attitude toward the facts is a greater threat to truth than outright lying.

A brief history lesson might prove instructive. Early in its life, the church encountered a great teacher of Mistruth 3; his name was Marcion (85–160 BCE). If not the first, he was the most famous and most compelling voice (at least up to that point) asserting that the Old Testament had been rendered permanently obsolete. It is noteworthy that one of his main works was entitled "The Antitheses." Marcion was an effective preacher and encouraged Bible study among his followers. As young as it was, the early church immediately recognized the threat Marcion posed.

He was excommunicated for his views and his teachings were extensively refuted by some of the best early Christian thinkers. These individuals demonstrated repeatedly and effectively that Marcion didn't know the whole truth about Scripture but only part of it. Still further, according to them, Marcion's heresy not only ruined the Old Testament, it did the same to the New, in part because Marcion produced a version of the New Testament that was vastly different than our own. It didn't have all four Gospels but only one. Marcion, evidently, wasn't very comfortable with complexity. One is far easier to deal with than four. Marcion definitely couldn't handle Matthew's Gospel, which is often seen as the most Jewish of the four, because, at root, Marcion was anti-Jewish. Also, as I've noted more than once already, Matthew repeatedly states that things in his Gospel happened in order to fulfill what was written in the Old Testament. That kind of cross-testament linkage, citing the Old Testament in support no less, was way too pro-Old Testament for Marcion. In the end, Marcion could only stomach Luke's Gospel, but even that was too much for him. He removed the opening chapters, which discuss Jesus' birth, in part because they are just too "Old Testament-ish." Those chapters sound very much like the stories about Sarah and Hannah, struggling with fertility, hoping for a long-awaited child. Marcion just couldn't take that. So he removed those chapters and edited Luke's Gospel in other ways too. He did the same with Paul's letters: he only included ten of those letters in his "version" of the New Testament and, again, altered them to remove as much Old Testament as possible.

Two things should be obvious from this brief history lesson: (1) as already pointed out in Mistruth 1, if you try to conduct a surgery like Marcion's on the New Testament, the patient simply won't survive the procedure. Marcion didn't have the New Testament—not like we do, at any rate.[4] All he had was a mutilated, censored, cut-and-paste version of what he liked in the New Testament. And that's a very different thing. No wonder the early church didn't like Marcion's approach and said thanks but no thanks. (2) Marcion's surgery was unsuccessful in another way: he just couldn't get all the Old Testament out of the New! The early church writers loved to demonstrate this, but even more pointedly, they drew attention to how Marcion's approach led to a whole host of theological problems: removing the Old Testament led to grave errors in Marcion's doctrine of God, his doctrine of Christ, his understanding of creation, human life, reproduction, and so on. If the Old Testament caused Marcion problems, the early church's response was, in so many words, "Your real problem was leaving the Old Testament behind in the first place." Marcion's "solution" caused far more problems than it solved.

Two final items should be mentioned with reference to Mistruth 3:

1. Even if Christians want to assert that much in the New Testament revises what is found in the Old Testament, that revision needn't be thought of as complete replacement or total erasure. What is on the books often stays on the books even if some new thing takes precedence for some reason. In our own political context this is clear from the Eighteenth Amendment to the Constitution of the United States, which prohibited "intoxicating liquors" in 1919, and which was subsequently repealed by the Twenty-First Amendment in 1933. The Eighteenth Amendment is still part of the Constitution even though it is no longer the law of the land given the Twenty-First. Revision, change, updating is simply not the same thing as total replacement, eradication, or obsolescence.

2. Why earlier material should remain on the books is in part due to the fact that close attention to it often

reveals much that is still worth pondering. The Eighteenth Amendment, for example, is still quite interesting, even if only for understanding a certain period of time in American history. Its place in the Constitution, including its repeal in the Twenty-First Amendment, is interesting since it is an instructive moment in the history of constitutional law that casts illuminating light on the nature of the Constitution of the United States (that it can be amended, for instance). The significance of certain Old Testament items that some Christians might deem "obsolete" (rightly or wrongly) is far greater still, if only because all of the Old Testament is "our mail" (see Mistruth 1).

The Temple, for instance, though not a location that we attend on a regular basis, is nevertheless worth pondering. Its decorative elements present it as a kind of microcosm of creation—or, perhaps better, the way creation is described is akin to the imagery found in the Temple. Studying the Temple, therefore, can be a spiritually enriching act, as it has been in that brand of Jewish mysticism known as Hekhalot mysticism. Or if we carefully consider sacrifice, we find that a great deal is going on in that practice beyond just bloody animal slaughter. In Deuteronomy, for instance, sacrifice is a way to support the Levites, who otherwise had no livelihood, and it is also an opportunity to provide for the poor and other disadvantaged members of society (see, e.g., Deut. 12:10–12). Leviticus offers a host of details about sacrifice, one of the most important of which is that there was more than one type of sacrifice (see chaps. 1–7). Not all sacrifice concerned sin and its forgiveness, and it was definitely not limited to only intentional wrongdoing. Some sacrifice was to repay vows or simply to give thanks to God. Whatever the case, sacrifice was designed to unify the worshiper and God, to make them "at one" (which is where we get the word "atone"). That is a goal that—however achieved—should never go out of style or ever be considered "obsolete."

CLARIFICATION 3:
The Old Testament is and remains a lively and useful part of Scripture and a crucial resource for Christian reflection.

QUESTIONS FOR DISCUSSION

1. Have you ever thought that the Old Testament was obsolete? On what basis? In light of this chapter, how "new" is the New Testament?
2. Does it matter to you that things in the New Testament are "new" or somehow deemed "better" than the Old Testament? Why or why not?
3. Had you heard of Marcion before reading this book? Have you ever noticed Marcionite tendencies (even if you didn't know Marcion's name) in others? In yourself?
4. In addition to the Temple and sacrifice, can you think of other topics "still on the books" in the Old Testament that are particularly useful for Christians to ponder?
5. What's in a name? Would it help to call the Old Testament something else, like "the First Testament" or just "The Bible"?

THE OLD TESTAMENT GOD IS MEAN . . .
REALLY MEAN

If Mistruth 3 was a doozy, so is Mistruth 4, though in a different way. Mistruth 4 is also vast, not so much in scope as in the malevolent spread of this particular piece of misinformation. Even Christians who like the Old Testament might still opine, at least occasionally, that the "Old Testament God" is mean. As for those who don't like the Old Testament, this opinion is usually front and center, perhaps first on the list of why they don't care for it. Boring is one thing (Mistruth 2), vicious is something else altogether.

There are at least two items people have in mind when they think about or perpetuate this mistruth: the first has to do with particular instances of violence in the Old Testament that are, in one way or another, connected to God. The parade example here is the conquest of Canaan. I treat this and similar issues in Mistruth 5. The second item is the more general problem of God's wrath or judgment. This is the matter I treat here as Mistruth 4, although there is considerable overlap between Mistruths 4 and 5 such that they might ultimately need to be thought about together.

As is the case with many of the other mistruths, the problem with Mistruth 4 is not that it is completely wide of the mark, though it is certainly the case that it is not on target either. Said differently, the problem with Mistruth 4 is that the information it contains is *mis*information because it is only partial, not as full as it should be or as full as it *needs* to be to tell the whole truth about the Old Testament—in this case, the whole truth about the Old Testament God.

Let's start with that very language: "the Old Testament God." At the very least, that way of putting things implies a difference that can be drawn between how God is portrayed in the Old Testament versus how God is portrayed in the New Testament. At the very most (and at its very worst) that way of putting things suggests that the God of the Old Testament is different than the "New Testament God." This "New Testament God," presumably, is associated with Jesus. But the New Testament itself, and Christian theology following suit, goes to great lengths to make clear that the God of Israel *is* the God and Father of the Lord Jesus Christ. Two Testaments, one God. To misunderstand this connection—this *fundamental identification*—is basically to belong to Marcion's camp, which is not a good place to be (see Mistruth 3).

This, then, is the first important point that must be entered about Mistruth 4: whatever we say about God in the Old Testament will have to be predicated, also, of God in the New. This is not only a literary assertion or some sort of canonical recommendation, it is *required* by orthodox Trinitarian theology, which says that the Three are One—so much so that where one of the members of the Trinity is present, so also are the other two (see also Mistruth 10). They operate inseparably. So, if the "Old Testament God" is mean . . . *really* mean, so is the "New Testament God," and so also is Christ and the Holy Spirit. There is no "divide and conquer" when it comes to the Trinity!

Now Mistruth 4 speaks both of God's *meanness* and its relative strength: *really mean*. Let's take each in order.

1. From the start, we should be careful to not sugarcoat the situation. There really is a good deal of divine wrath in the Old Testament and there can be no doubt that it often makes modern readers uncomfortable—and that it takes violent forms (see Mistruth 5). But before going any further, it must be stressed that there is a good bit of divine wrath (and violence) in the New Testament too, and not just in the story of Jesus driving people out of the Temple with a whip (I doubt he was smiling when he did this) or in the gruesome end-times violence one reads in the book of Revelation (if one ever gets around to reading it). A close look at any of the Gospels shows that they are chock-full of parables and statements that show Jesus to be a comfortable and expert preacher of divine judgment (e.g., to stick with just Luke, see 13:1–5; 16:19–31; 21:20–24; 23:29–31; and Jesus' cousin John was good at it too: see 3:7–9). That means that Jesus was also a comfortable and expert preacher of divine wrath since these two—divine judgment and divine wrath—go hand in hand.

This last point is decisive: *divine judgment and divine wrath go together*. To put the matter in other words, we can say that, in Scripture, when God is angry, God is angry about something. It is crucial, as the great twentieth-century rabbi Abraham Joshua Heschel observed, to distinguish between "the wrath of God" (*ira Dei*) and "the God of wrath" (*Deus irae*).[1] The latter formulation suggests that God *is* wrathful as a matter of course, as part of the divine nature, maybe even always. The former way of putting things, by way of contrast, indicates that wrath is something God has *about something*. God's wrath, in other words, takes an object. When that "something" that makes God mad changes, then so does God's wrath: it, too, changes— it dissipates, disappears, relents. God is no longer wrathful when that "something" is taken care of; God is now in some other state of being: pleased, perhaps, maybe even happy. The purpose that motivates the prophetic preaching of repentance, whether it's Amos and Ezekiel or Jesus and John the Baptist, is to change the listener's ways. When that change is accomplished, the listener moves from being an object of divine wrath (even if only potentially) to being an object of divine favor (in reality). When it comes to divine judgment and wrath, human change changes God (see, e.g., Jer. 3:12–14; 18:7–10; Jonah 3:10). As Ezekiel puts it, God takes no joy in judgment:

> As I live, says the Lord GOD, I have no pleasure in the death of the wicked, but that the wicked turn from their ways and live; turn back, turn back from your evil ways; for why will you die, O house of Israel? (Ezek. 33:11; see also 18:21–23)

Jesus agrees:

> God didn't send his Son into the world to judge the world, but that the world might be saved through him. (John 3:17 CEB)

Fine and good, but the question that follows, then, is *what*, exactly, is God mad about in the Bible? Two things, mainly: injustice and sin. Rabbi Heschel is again worth quoting at length:

> The wrath of God is a lamentation. All prophecy is one great exclamation: God is not indifferent to evil! He is always concerned, He is personally affected by what man does to man. He is a God of pathos. This is one of the meanings of the anger of God: the end of indifference![2]

And so the Prophets came preaching divine wrath and judgment—*unto repentance*! And so Jesus and John the

Baptist and all the rest came preaching the same—*unto repentance!* They came preaching the wrath and judgment of God (since these go hand in hand): a lamentation, an exclamation, an end to indifference, an end to injustice and sin.

The chance to change is why the Prophets and the apostles and all the rest preach about God's judgment and wrath, which take as their object the malign twins injustice and sin. What that means, in so many words, is that this aspect of the Old Testament (and "the Old Testament God") that many Christians dislike so strongly is, in the final analysis, a benevolent, even therapeutic conception. The fact that many Christians would dislike this benevolent, even therapeutic notion—that God is mobilized against injustice and sin—says a great deal about them (er, I mean, *us*). In fact, I think it says more about them (that is, *us*) than it does about the Old Testament (and the New) and its portrayal of God. To put a fine point on it: perhaps we don't like divine judgment and wrath, wherever we find it in Scripture, because we are perfectly comfortable with injustice and sin, because we—unlike God—are indifferent to evil. Perhaps this also explains why so many Christians seem completely tone-deaf to the notes of divine judgment Jesus continually sounds, favoring instead a sanitized, anesthetized, milquetoast vision of Jesus as some sort of approachable coach figure or well-intentioned boyfriend that is full of nothing but "love." Here's just one example from a familiar and well-beloved passage that showcases Jesus' penchant for judgment:

> I am the true vine, and my Father is the vinegrower.
> He removes every branch in me that bears no fruit.
> Every branch that bears fruit he prunes to make it
> bear more fruit. You have already been cleansed by
> the word that I have spoken to you. Abide in me
> as I abide in you. Just as the branch cannot bear
> fruit by itself unless it abides in the vine, neither can

you unless you abide in me. I am the vine, you are the branches. Those who abide in me and I in them bear much fruit, because apart from me you can do nothing. Whoever does not abide in me is thrown away like a branch and withers; such branches are gathered, thrown into the fire, and burned. (John 15:1–6)

To repeat: Such branches, Jesus says, *are thrown into the fire and burned*; those branches are *not* loved or cared for or forgiven or some other syrupy-sweet cliché that blunts the double-edged sword coming out of his mouth. The uber-famous passage from John 3 is not unrelated:

For God so loved the world that he gave his only Son, so that everyone who believes in him may not perish but may have eternal life. Indeed, God did not send the Son into the world to condemn the world, but in order that the world might be saved through him. Those who believe in him are not condemned; but those who do not believe are condemned already, because they have not believed in the name of the only Son of God. (John 3:16–18)

To repeat: Those who do not believe, Jesus says, *are already condemned*; those who do not believe are *not* saved or redeemed or whatever. Perhaps because the people who do not believe and who are condemned already are those who are comfortable with and indifferent to injustice and sin, or, to use the language of the next verse, because they are people who "loved darkness rather than light because their deeds were evil" (3:19).

"Love" as a divine quality needs some serious nuancing, therefore. Walker Percy says the word *love* "has been polluted. Beware of people who go around talking about loving and caring."[3] "Love" doesn't really mean what we think it means; perhaps it would be best to not use the word for a while. In the case of the Bible, God's "love" does not come without at least a fine silvery lacing of judgment, and sometimes the lacing in that "love" is not fine at all but substantial, undiscriminating, unavoidable. It might not be going too far to say that, in the Bible (*both* Testaments), God's judgment is an instance of God's love: it is the chance to change and be restored. Again, Heschel puts it best: "The call of anger is a call to cancel anger. . . . For all its intensity, it may be averted by prayer. There is no divine anger for anger's sake" because "the secret of anger is God's care."[4] In brief, we ignore and/or dislike divine judgment and wrath to our own peril—our own detriment! What's not to like about the chance to change, the chance to be free of injustice and sin, the chance to be right with God?

2. All well and good, but what about the question of relative strength: *just how angry* is God in the Old Testament? Psalm 7:11 would indicate that instances of God's anger are not infrequent:

> God is a righteous judge,
> and a God who has indignation every day.

Being angry every day is . . . well, *a lot*! Of course, if what God is angry about is injustice and sin, there's no real surprise here. We all know—deeply and intimately—how common injustice and sin are in our world . . . and in our hearts. The connection between God's anger and its usual objects is presented with greater clarity in the freer translation of Psalm 7:11 that is found in the Common English Bible:

> God is a righteous judge,
> a God who is angry *at evil* every single day.
> (CEB, italics added)

This translation is supported by the larger biblical witness regarding God's anger—specifically, the particular targets of divine wrath and judgment.

The larger biblical witness is also what led the rabbis to some fascinating interpretations replete with mathematical calculations. The rabbis considered texts like Psalm 7:11 in concert with texts like Isaiah 54:7–8:

> For a brief moment I abandoned you,
> but with great compassion I will gather you.
> In overflowing wrath for a moment
> I hid my face from you,
> but with everlasting love I will have compassion
>   on you,
> says the LORD, your Redeemer.

So, yes, God is angry every day, the rabbis reasoned—that's what Psalm 7:11 reports—but *how long* is God angry every day? Isaiah 54, they noted, suggests that divine anger is only for the briefest of moments. So, yes, everyday divine wrath but for a very short period of time. How short? According to the rabbis' final calculation, based on how long they thought "a moment" was in Hebrew, God's everyday anger lasts only 0.06 seconds.[5] Now that might be enough time to determine gold from silver in the Olympic games but it is impossibly short in the lived experience of a twenty-four-hour day.

In the same context, the rabbis commented on the phrase "house of my prayer" in Isaiah 56:7, which, in a wooden construal, seems to suggest that the Lord also prays. To whom would the Lord pray? And about what? The rabbis didn't shy away from answering these questions. According to them, God prays to himself (!) the following prayer every day: "May it be My will that My mercy may suppress My anger, and that My mercy may prevail over My [other] attributes, so that I may deal with My children in the attribute of mercy and, on their behalf, stop short of the limit of strict justice."[6]

In sum: Angry? Yes (for approximately 0.06 seconds per day, give or take a nanosecond). Mean? Not so much. *Really* mean? No, not really. Helpfully, maybe even salvifically angry about things that really matter? *Most definitely.*

CLARIFICATION 4:
God in Scripture (not just the Old Testament) is deeply upset about injustice and sin; God's judgment of those things is in service to setting the world aright.

QUESTIONS FOR DISCUSSION:

1. Have you ever thought that the Old Testament and New Testament were at complete odds when it came to divine wrath? On what basis did you think this?
2. Do you find the wrath of God troubling in the Old Testament but not the New? Why?
3. Have you ever considered Jesus to be wrathful? Why or why not? Why would Jesus be angry? What would he be angry about? Have a look at Mark 1:41, where many early Greek manuscripts of the New Testament state that Jesus was moved "with anger"—not pity—when he cleansed the leper. The CEB translates this verse as: "Incensed, Jesus reached out his hand, touched him, and said, 'I do want to. Be clean.'" Why do we so often miss Jesus' comments that are full of wrath or anger?

4. Sometimes we use phrases like "righteous indignation" to soften the notion of divine anger over sin and injustice. Is that a good move?

5. Is it possible that we are uncomfortable with divine wrath and judgment because we do not want to face our own complicity with and indifference toward injustice and sin?

THE OLD TESTAMENT IS HYPER-VIOLENT

As I noted in the previous chapter, Mistruths 4 and 5 go together in many ways. The "meanness" of God in the Old Testament is often located mostly, if not exclusively, in violent actions attributed to God in Scripture—in *both* Testaments (read Revelation, in the case of the New, if you haven't already; chapters 18–19 should do the trick). In the preceding discussion, I filleted the issue by treating God's "mean" side with reference to the question of divine judgment, reserving violence for the discussion of Mistruth 5. Quite apart from portrayals of God or divine judgment, the Old Testament has plenty of violent, even gruesome passages. The judge Ehud's killing of Eglon, for instance, comes to mind and is quite graphic:

> Ehud reached with his left hand and grabbed the sword from his right thigh. He stabbed it into Eglon's stomach, and even the handle went in after the blade. Since he did not pull the sword out of his stomach, the fat closed over the blade, and his guts spilled out. (Judg. 3:21–22 CEB)

Or there's David beheading Goliath with his own sword (1 Sam. 17:51), the dogs licking up the blood of Ahab and the prostitutes bathing in it (1 Kgs. 22:38); Jezebel's being thrown from a tower with her blood splattering all over and her corpse being devoured (2 Kgs. 9:30–37); and so on and so forth. And that's really just the tip of the iceberg.

That big (and rather bloody) iceberg explains the following exchange I recently overheard at a middle-school soccer game:

A mother (speaking to her elementary-school-aged son): "I saw a funny thing today. It was a cartoon that said, 'After researchers determine violent video games are bad for school-aged boys, parents decide to have their children read the Old Testament instead.'"

Son: "Wait, what?"

(Mom repeats.)

Son: "I don't get it."

(Mom repeats with a bit more explanation this time — pointing out that the Old Testament is violent.)

Although it took the boy a few times to get the joke, he eventually got it. Since I'm an Old Testament professor by training and by choice, the joke caused me to wince a bit — well, maybe more than a bit; I may have had to bite my tongue. But I have to admit it *is* kind of funny. The joke is also more than a bit revealing: not just about the Old Testament, but also about our knowledge of the Bible and about our own proclivities to violence. Let me unpack each of these elements but not without first noting, even if only in passing, that the son didn't initially get the joke. He had to be *taught* this particular mistruth. As I said in the Introduction to this book: *somebody* told us the things we've been misled to believe about the Old Testament. Sometimes it's a parent as much as a preacher or church teacher of whatever sort.

1. So, first, as the four brief examples from Judges, Samuel, 1 Kings, and 2 Kings demonstrate, there is cer-

tainly a good bit of violence in the Bible—the mom's joke gets its punchline from that fact. There is no misinformation going on, therefore, in that part of Mistruth 5: The Old Testament *is* violent. Well . . . actually, let me take that back. To return to the distinction that Heschel drew for us with regard to the difference between the "God of wrath" and "God having wrath" (see Mistruth 4), it would be far more accurate to say that the Old Testament *has* (some) violence in it, not that it *is* violent per se, consistently and constantly. Quite to the contrary, the Old Testament has a great deal of *non*violence in it, starting with the peaceful creation of the world by God, which is in marked contrast to the frequently violent portrayals of creation known from contemporaneous ancient Near Eastern accounts, and by the fact that the diet of both animals and human beings in the beginning was strictly vegetarian (see Gen. 1:29–30). The Old Testament's vision of the future is also marked by peace and lack of conflict and strife (Isa. 11:1–9; 66:17–25; Zech. 8:1–8; etc.). This arc of nonviolence indicates that something "in between" the peaceful bookends has gone terribly wrong; the "in-between" is marked by violence, but it was not originally so, neither is it to be so, again, in the end. So, the Old Testament *has* violence in it, to be sure, but the Old Testament is not in and of itself violent, and certainly not always. The Old Testament's origin and ending lie decidedly with peace, not with violence, as do a number of other Old Testament moments along the way. Mistruth 5 needs serious correction, therefore, and we haven't even gotten to the bit about *hyper*-violent. So, is the Old Testament violent? Sure, *sometimes*. But the Old Testament is also *nonviolent* sometimes. Much depends on which times are which!

2. Second, the joke is revealing by associating violence with the Old Testament alone. Why doesn't the punch line say that parents are having their children read the Old Testament and the New Testament? Or why not just the

New Testament alone? The answer, I suspect, is because the cartoonist doesn't think the New Testament is violent, at least not like the Old Testament. But, as I've pointed out in the case of Mistruths 3 and 4, this "divide-and-conquer" approach to the Bible is not only unhelpful, it's also inaccurate, if not actually heretical (see the discussion of Marcion in Mistruth 3). The New Testament, too, has its fair share of violence—the issue of divine wrath and judgment in the preaching of Jesus is an obvious case in point (see Mistruth 4). But violence is also found in Paul's letters, like in this passage from 2 Thessalonians:

> This is evidence of the righteous judgment of God, and is intended to make you worthy of the kingdom of God, for which you are also suffering. For it is indeed just of God to repay with affliction those who afflict you, and to give relief to the afflicted as well as to us, when the Lord Jesus is revealed from heaven with his mighty angels in flaming fire, inflicting vengeance on those who do not know God and on those who do not obey the gospel of our Lord Jesus. These will suffer the punishment of eternal destruction, separated from the presence of the Lord and from the glory of his might, when he comes to be glorified by his saints and to be marveled at on that day among all who have believed, because our testimony to you was believed. To this end we always pray for you, asking that our God will make you worthy of his call and will fulfill by his power every good resolve and work of faith, so that the name of our Lord Jesus may be glorified in you, and you in him, according to the grace of our God and the Lord Jesus Christ. (2 Thess. 1:5–12)

The violence in this case is *eschatological*—it concerns the end of the world and final judgment, which is also the kind of violence that marks the book of Revelation. Given the ultimate nature of all that, it doesn't seem to be going too far to say that the violence in the New Testament, especially in eschatological scenarios like Revelation or this passage from 2 Thessalonians, *rivals if not surpasses* anything found in the Old Testament. I mean, dying is one thing. But "the second death" (Rev. 20:14; 21:8)? Now *that's* brutal! That at least sounds far more violent than the Old Testament. Maybe it's the New Testament that is hyper-violent!

I do not mean to appear snide about these things. Neither am I trying to disparage the New Testament. (The only thing worse than grappling with the fact that the Old Testament is violent is to learn that the New Testament is violent too!) Rather, my point is that on this matter—in the case of this mistruth—as also with so many others Christians wrestle with when thinking about the Old Testament, the two Testaments are united: united in the problems they pose and also in the solutions they offer. It would not be wise, nor accurate, to think that the problems Scripture poses for modern Christian readers in the twenty-first century reside only in the Old Testament. No. For better or for worse, the problems also reside in the New. Christians need to think hard and holistically about the entirety of Scripture when engaging difficult questions like violence, or when they are trying to evaluate tricky mistruths like "The Old Testament is hyper-violent."

All well and good, but, again, we mustn't sugarcoat things. We turn now to the most violent and difficult of the Bible's violent moments according to many people—the conquest of Canaan. A lot of people see this as nothing less than what we would call in our world *genocide*: "The deliberate and systematic extermination of an ethnic or national group."[1] Any number of texts from Joshua could be cited at this point, since that is where the conquest is mostly recounted, but let's consider an equally exemplary (and disturbing) passage from Deuteronomy 7.

> Now once the LORD your God brings you into the land you are entering to take possession of, and he drives out numerous nations before you—the Hittites, the Girgashites, the Amorites, the Canaanites, the Perizzites, the Hivites, and the Jebusites: seven nations that are larger and stronger than you—once the LORD your God lays them before you, you must strike them down, placing them under the ban. Don't make any covenants with them, and don't be merciful to them. Don't intermarry with them. Don't give your daughter to one of their sons to marry, and don't take one of their daughters to marry your son, because they will turn your child away from following me so that they end up serving other gods. That will make the LORD's anger burn against you, and he will quickly annihilate you. Instead, this is what you must do with these nations: rip down their altars, smash their sacred stones, cut down their sacred poles, and burn their idols because you are a people holy to the LORD your God. The LORD your God chose you to be his own treasured people beyond all others on the fertile land. It was not because you were greater than all other people that the LORD loved you and chose you. In fact, you were the smallest of peoples! (Deut. 7:1–7; CEB)

What CEB translates as "placing them under the ban" (v. 2) is rendered in the NRSV as "then you must utterly destroy them" and in the New Jewish Publication Society Version (NJPSV) as "you must doom them to destruction." Is the CEB's translation sanitized somehow, censored in some way, a case of wishful thinking (at best) or deliberate misleading (at worst)?

Hardly. In Hebrew, the key phrase is an emphatic construction comprised of two words that both come from the same verbal root, *ḥ-r-m* (the entire phrase sounds roughly like *ḥacharaym tachareem*), which means something like "devote to destruction," especially in militaristic contexts, but which can also mean something like "set aside" or mark as "off limits." NRSV and NJPSV incline toward the destructive sense in Deuteronomy 7:2, in part because the passage concerns life on the other side of the Jordan in the land of Canaan—a long-term settlement process, often marked by militaristic action, that is discussed in further detail in Joshua and Judges. But does the phrase really mean "utterly destroy" or "doom to destruction" in Deuteronomy 7:2?

The answer to that question would appear to be "no," if only because covenants are not made with people who are already dead, nor are marriages entered into with corpses. If *ḥacharaym tachareem* specifies an act of genocide, then there would be no one left alive to covenant with, no survivors to get married to—those commandments are entirely unnecessary if genocide was the only and obvious meaning of *ḥacharaym tachareem*. These considerations (among others) lie behind the CEB's translation. "Placing under the ban" is less specific in terms of what the phrase actually means but is perhaps more accurate for the very same reason. What the "ban" means needs further exploration and discussion, to be sure. And there can be no doubt that, according to Joshua, the conquest of Canaan involved a good bit of militaristic destruction. But maybe there is a hint here already in Deuteronomy 7 and in "the ban" itself—two parade examples of the violence of the Canaanite conquest—that more is going on than meets the eye. Maybe Deuteronomy 7 and "the ban" is about far more (or, better, far *less*) than genocide.[2]

More time and more texts would add further weight to this interpretation. Genocide, by definition, is thoroughgoing and unremitting. What happens in Joshua is far from that, decidedly *otherwise*. We hear again and again of "exceptions to the anti-Canaanite clause," to coin a phrase. Rahab and her family, for instance (see Josh. 2:9–13; 6:25), or the story of the covenant made with the Gibeonites (9:1–27), are stories showing how certain Canaanite groups successfully avoid "the ban" (whatever it is) and become incorporated into Israel. And then there are numerous notifications in the book of Joshua that the situation on the ground at that time was *complex*, to say the least. These passages convey the clear impression that the conquest was *not* entirely effective, thoroughgoing, or wide-ranging. Texts like Joshua 13:1–7; 15:63; 16:10; 17:12–13; and 23:5–13 show that much land was *un*conquered and various people groups were *not* eliminated, with many living among Israel, even in Jerusalem (!), "to this day."

In this regard, it may be observed that the conquest of Canaan *begins* with the curious encounter between Joshua and the commander of the Lord's army (Josh. 5:13–15). When Joshua asks which side the commander is on, the answer is "Neither!" That's almost certainly *not* the answer Joshua wanted to hear, on the cusp of the Israelites' first military engagement in Canaan, but it seems to demonstrate, if nothing else, that God does not show favoritism (Deut. 10:17; Acts 10:34; Rom. 2:11; Eph. 6:9)—not even in the conquest—and that God has other sheep that are not solely from the flock of Israel (John 10:16; see also Amos 9:7). In fact, those sheep may even include Canaanites, as evidenced by Rahab, the Gibeonites, and other "exceptions," including the amazing story of Jesus' exchange with a *Canaanite* woman, who came to him pleading on behalf of her demon-possessed daughter (Matt. 15:21–28). Canaanites were still running around, evidently, a thousand years after Joshua and the Israelites "conquered" Canaan! In this story in Matthew 15, therefore, if nowhere else, lies definitive proof that the Lord himself sanctions exceptions to the anti-Canaanite clause: Jesus says, "'Woman, great is your faith! Let it be done for you as you wish.' And her daughter was healed instantly" (Matt. 15:28).

Details like the ones I've just mentioned do not solve the problem of violence in the Bible. Of course they don't. Violence is still present in the Bible, no doubt because the Bible tells true stories about human beings, a violent race to be sure (see below; Isa. 5:7; Gen. 6:6; 8:21). But details like the ones I've mentioned nevertheless help to *limit* violence. These details (and others that might be mentioned) demonstrate that neither the Old Testament nor the New *is* violent, intrinsically or consistently. They also show that the violence found in Scripture may be different than what we are accustomed to.

That brings me to another important thing that the joke at the soccer game reveals—namely, *how violent we are*. We all know that video games can be violent. But so can movies and TV shows, even music on the radio. All of the violence I just named is violence we use *for our own entertainment*. Who's *hyper*-violent now? If we are offended by the Bible's violence, it is possible that the Bible (personified for a moment) might look back at us and say: "Who are you calling violent?" Our own brands of violence are far more graphic, more brutal, and more effective than anything the biblical authors could ever have imagined. Death by sword is one thing, but the biblical authors had no extended magazines, armor-piercing bullets, carpet bombs, biological and chemical weapons, or nuclear warheads to cause maximum damage, killing the most amount of people with minimal physical effort. Neither did the biblical authors spend their hard-earned money and leisure time on entertaining themselves with violence. Quite to the contrary, it seems that *the Bible itself is concerned about violence* and does what it can to limit the violence it does contain in significant ways. The conquest of Canaan, for instance, is limited to *back then* and *back there*—under Joshua, at a particular period of time, in a specific location, and for particular reasons that were of divine not human origin. The conquest does not reappear as a dominant experience or metaphor for the people of God during the exodus from Egypt or the exile to Babylon, which are referenced frequently in Scripture as key moments and images in the life of faith.

A few additional words, especially about the divine origin of much biblical violence, are in order. On the one hand, the divine origin of biblical violence is hardly a comforting thought: doesn't it just punt the problem further down the line by suggesting that *God* is the hyper-violent entity in question? Well, not exactly in light of what was said about Mistruth 4. In Scripture, we must recall, God is angry *about something*—injustice and sin mostly. And, whether we like it or not, the Old Testament does, at least at some points, describe the prior inhabitants of the land as falling short of God's wishes. Already in Genesis 15, generations before Joshua, God tells Abram that his descendants will be slaves for four hundred years before taking possession of the land. Only after that extended period of time will they return to the land "since the Amorites' wrongdoing won't have reached its peak until then" (Gen. 15:16 CEB). This verse, as brief and as obscure as it is, suggests that God's delay in bringing the promise of land to fulfillment is connected to the wickedness of the land's inhabitants (here called Amorites). That must reach its full measure, according to this verse, which suggests, in turn, that the conquest is a punishment for that full wickedness. Over in Leviticus, God warns Israel to not follow various practices of the Canaanites, which made the land unclean to the point that the ground itself vomited them out (Lev. 18:24–30; 20:22–27). In Deuteronomy, the divinely mandated rules of war require that peaceful terms should be offered to an enemy city before any military engagement (20:10). It is perhaps no surprise that the "exceptions" in Joshua have heard of the Lord's acts and, in turn, act accordingly (see Josh. 2:9–13; 9:3; cf. Ps. 111:10). Neither is it a surprise that the Canaanite woman who comes to Jesus thrice calls him "Lord," and begs him for mercy. And that is what she is shown.

To sum up: Is the violence that remains in the Old Testament a matter of concern? Most definitely. But is the Old Testament violent for violence's sake, even hyper-violent? Most definitely not. Our own violence, by way of contrast, seems *limitless*. Talk about hyper.

Much, much more could be said about Mistruth 5, but at the end of the day, maybe one way to approach the violence found in Scripture is by battling another, widespread mistruth about the Old Testament (and the Bible as a whole)—namely, "Everything in the Bible Is Meant to Be Replicated or Imitated." Although I haven't included a treatment of this mistruth in the present book, it's a pervasive one that is not unrelated to the matter at hand and that must be challenged and set right. The Bible is full of passages, stories, poems, and so forth that are nothing like moral exhortation. Such texts are not *prescriptive*, mandating or encouraging certain behavior, so much as they are *descriptive*, describing something that happened. Lessons may be learned or taken from such descriptions, to be sure, but that is a very different thing (and a very different interpretive exercise) than a text containing a straightforward command like: "Love your neighbor as yourself" (Lev. 19:18b) or "Pray without ceasing" (1 Thess. 5:17).

Furthermore, learning from a description of something that happened in the past is not the same as actively recreating it and doing it now. Descriptive texts that tell of some happening, like, say the conquest of Canaan, may be quite informative, maybe even formative in some fashion (as a cautionary tale, perhaps, or as narrating some important theological and ethical point), without inviting, let alone requiring, us to "go and do likewise." In fact, any formation involved with descriptive texts may be entirely by way of *contrast*, saying something like the following:

> Do *not* go out and do likewise, because that was limited to *back then* and *back there*. Plus, there were exceptions. And, besides that, there are important prescriptive texts to consider that aren't limited— ones like "Love your neighbor as yourself" (Lev. 19:18b) and "love [the immigrant] as yourself, because you were immigrants in the land of Egypt" (Lev. 19:34 CEB).

Now those are some lessons to learn and replicate!

CLARIFICATION 5:
Both Testaments — Old *and* New — contain violent passages; violence is not, however, part of God's initial purposes in creation, nor is it the end goal of the divine plan. Instead, the Bible manifests attempt to limit and constrain violence, encouraging us to contain our own proclivities to hyper-violence.

QUESTIONS FOR DISCUSSION

1. Have you ever considered the New Testament to contain violent passages? Why not? Does this say something about your level of familiarity with the New Testament or a certain tendency to divide the Testaments when things get tricky?
2. Are the various ideas and texts mentioned in this chapter helpful in assessing the difficult problem of

violence in the Bible? Which ideas or texts are most helpful to you and how so?

3. Can you identify other ways the Old Testament and New Testament limit or constrain violence?

4. Do you agree that we are violent now? If not, why not? And if not, what, then, do you make of so much evidence to the contrary in our culture and our leisure pursuits?

5. Can you imagine ways that the Bible's own constraints on violence might be used to limit our own brands of violence now?

DAVID WROTE THE PSALMS (AND OTHER UNHELPFUL HISTORICAL ASSERTIONS)

Most Christians know that David wrote the Psalms. Or at least that's one of the lies that someone has told us along the way. Or, more generously, it's one of the *mistruths* we've picked up along the way. Whatever we call it, this assertion, and several others like it, just ain't so.

Why not? For several reasons:

1. First, nowhere in the Bible are we told "David wrote the Psalms." Why, then, would someone tell us that he did? Well, because we *are* told in some places in the Bible that certain psalms trace back somehow to David. A parade example is found in Jesus's own words, in an exchange with the Pharisees in Matthew 22:

> Now as the Pharisees were gathering, Jesus asked them, "What do you think about the Christ? Whose son is he?" "David's son," they replied. He said, "Then how is it that David, inspired by the Holy Spirit, called him Lord when he said, The Lord said to my lord, 'Sit at my right side until I turn your enemies into your footstool'? If David calls him Lord, how can he be David's son?" Nobody was able to

answer him. And from that day forward nobody dared to ask him anything. (Matt. 22:41–46 CEB; see also Mark 12:35–37; Luke 20:41–44)

Here, in a nifty if not also tricky little piece of biblical interpretation, Jesus cites Psalm 110:1 (see also Ps. 8:6b) to show that the Christ (Messiah) is discussed by "David, inspired by the Holy Spirit." The point of Jesus' citation of the psalm is that the Messiah is not *just* the son of David in terms of genealogy, but much more than that. Those who were watching evidently got Jesus' drift just fine: "And the large crowd was listening to him with delight," Mark says (12:37). For our purposes, however, the point is that Jesus cites Psalm 110 and says it was spoken by David.

Outside of the Gospels, we read of Peter citing Psalm 69:25 and Psalm 109:8, calling it "the scripture . . . which the Holy Spirit through David foretold" (Acts 1:16). A chapter later, in his great Pentecost sermon, Peter does more of the same, this time citing Psalm 16:8–11 after introducing the quotation with "For David says concerning him" (Acts 2:25–28; see also v. 31). And just one sermon point later, Peter does his best Jesus imitation by citing Psalm 110:1, stating that that verse is something David "himself says" (Acts 2:34–35). A few chapters later, the believers, in the middle of prayer, cite Psalm 2:1–2, attributing it to David, sort of, but also to God through the Spirit:

When they heard it, they raised their voices together to God and said, "Sovereign Lord, who made the heaven and the earth, the sea, and everything in them, it is you who said by the Holy Spirit through our ancestor David, your servant . . . (Acts 4:24–25)

Paul does much the same thing, not in a prayer, but in a sermon in Antioch (Acts 16:35), this time with reference to Psalm 16:10. In this case, like Acts 4, it is unclear if Paul credits the speaking of the psalm to God (see vv. 33–34) or David (see v. 36). There is no doubt at all that Paul attributes Psalm 32:1–2 to David in Romans 4:6–8, and that he does the same with Psalm 69:22–23 in Romans 11:9–10. The author of the Epistle to the Hebrews cites Psalm 95 a number of times, attributing the language to the Holy Spirit (3:7), God (4:3), and God "through David" (4:7).

This is impressive testimony, to be sure, though it is also clear that the testimony isn't entirely uniform: the witnesses waffle a bit—is the psalm in question to be attributed to David or God? If push came to shove, they'd likely default to the latter. Furthermore, even when the attribution does go to David, that famous king is frequently said to be speaking with the help of the Holy Spirit, in a kind of prophetic mode. Regardless of that point, the testimony given above seems to support what I am calling the *mis*-truth of "David wrote the Psalms." Why, then, call it a mistruth? That leads to the second point.

2. There are a good number of psalms that do not have anything to do with David. They do not mention him in the body of the psalm nor in the introductory line or two (called a superscription) that accompanies many, but not all, of the psalms. In fact, a number of these superscriptions mention *other* people, not David. *If* these superscriptions are meant to somehow indicate authorship—and that is a very big "if" (see the next point below)—then these non-Davidic psalms *disprove* that "David wrote (all) the Psalms" because, well, he obviously didn't. Some of these psalms are attributed to the sons of Korah (see, e.g., Ps. 42), others to Asaph (e.g., Ps. 50), another to Heman the Ezrahite and another to Ethan the Ezrahite (Pss. 88–89), another to Moses (Ps. 90), and two to Solomon (Pss. 72, 127). Psalm 102 is prefaced with "A prayer of one afflicted, when faint and pleading before the LORD." A number of psalms mention someone called "the leader," though the vast majority of these usually also mention David in some way, with

Psalm 39 including "Jeduthun," making the duet a trio. Then there are the psalms that don't have any mention of anybody whatsoever in their superscriptions or that lack superscriptions altogether.

This second point is important, but, even so, there remain quite a few superscriptions that mention David — beyond the ones that mention him and "the leader." These superscriptions are usually quite brief and come in various forms:

"A Psalm of David," "A Psalm of David, for the memorial offering," "A Miktam of David," "A Prayer of David," "A Maskil of David," or, most simply of all, just: "Of David."

Extended superscriptions that mention David, along with various contextual details, are atypical, but there are no less than twelve that do so, such as: "A Psalm of David, when he fled from his son Absalom" (Psalm 3); or "when Doeg the Edomite came to Saul and said to him, 'David has come to the house of Ahimelech'" (Ps. 52); or "when he struggled with Aram-naharaim and with Aram-zobah, and when Joab on his return killed twelve thousand Edomites in the Valley of Salt" (Ps. 60). The most famous of these twelve is the penitential Psalm 51:

> To the leader. A Psalm of David, when the prophet Nathan came to him, after he had gone in to Bathsheba.

There is no doubt that these extended superscriptions reflect (and create) fascinating connections between the psalm in question and some moment(s) in the life of David. But that doesn't mean that *all* of the Psalms must be associated with David or somehow placed in his life story. The superscription to Psalm 7, "A Shiggaion of David, which he sang to the Lord concerning Cush, a Benjaminite," for instance, doesn't fit with anything we know of David's life from Samuel, Kings, or Chronicles; and Psalm 52 seems to fit only loosely with 1 Samuel 21:1–8 and 22:6–19. Or consider Psalm 60: the superscription there seems to make it as much about Joab's life than David's.

3. This brings me to the third point that should be mentioned with regard to Mistruth 6: The particular Hebrew construction that is translated "of David" or "of Asaph," or anyone else, in English does not necessarily mean "authored by." The Hebrew construction could just as well mean "for David," as in *"dedicated to* David." Even the translation "of David" might mean something like "in *Davidic mode.*" The key superscription to consider in this regard is Psalm 30, which says "of David" but which is also explicitly said to be "A Psalm" and "A Song at the dedication of the temple." Here's the rub: David wasn't alive when the temple was completed (see 1 Kgs. 2:10–12; 6:1–38; 1 Chr. 29:26–28; 2 Chr. 3:1–5:1). Psalm 30 makes clear, then, that "of David" does not mean composed by David—not always at any rate. Even "the Davidic" psalms may not be authored by David.

But what about all those New Testament references? In almost every case, the psalms that the New Testament associates with David are psalms that do include some mention of David in their superscriptions. The New Testament references demonstrate that, by the first century, people seem to have understood "of David" to mean something like "by David," but maybe not entirely—if only because several of the New Testament references blur the ultimate "authorship" of the psalm in question: is it God or is it David? Even if it is David, God uttered it *through* David somehow, by the Holy Spirit, for example.

Now by this point in the chapter, amidst all these details and Psalm references, your head might be swimming and you might be asking yourself: What's the big deal about Mistruth 6 anyway? Who cares? Or why care about this as a major mistruth? *Is* it a major mistruth?

These are all good questions. I use the example of David authoring the Psalms as just one example of a larger mistruth—the one I am really most concerned with and that I include in the title of Mistruth 6 parenthetically: "and other unhelpful historical assertions." In the case of David and the Psalms, the unhelpful historical assertion is that David wrote all of them and that that should somehow inform, maybe even dictate our reading of the Psalms. Perhaps you, like me, have heard various sermons or lessons on this psalm or that, with a Davidic superscription or without (let alone one of the big twelve), that tried very, very hard to relate the specific psalm to some other text in the Bible about the life of David as if that were the point of the psalm. But of course, that is exactly *not* the point of the psalm. The point of the psalm—or, better, the *points* (plural) of the psalm, are found in the psalm itself, in what it says, not in something outside the psalm, some point in David's life known from Samuel or Kings or Chronicles, especially something that may not be able to be determined (e.g., Ps. 7), that fits at best only loosely (e.g., Ps. 52), or that doesn't fit at all (Ps. 30). Sure, you *can* relate the Psalms to David's life, especially with the twelve psalms that have extended Davidic superscriptions, but the Psalms have their own content, say their own things, make their own points quite apart from that and quite apart from the superscriptions. Exactly who authored the Psalms, when, where, how, and so on, is of far less importance than the words of the Psalms themselves. Surely that is part of what is going on when the New Testament authors go over David's head (even with "Davidic" psalms) and attribute the Psalms' ultimate origin to God. It is worth noting at this point that one of the New Testament texts that does this very thing, the Epistle to the Hebrews, is itself an *anonymous letter*. Sure, some people have attributed Hebrews to Paul (not unlike so many psalms are attributed "to David") but the letter doesn't mention Paul by name and so we really don't know who wrote it. But who wrote Hebrews isn't nearly as important as what Hebrews itself *says*. Not even close.

The underlying issue at work in Mistruth 6 is simply this: Many people hang their hats on exactly who wrote what in the Bible if not also exactly where and precisely when they did so. And so it is that many of us have been taught, not only that David wrote (all of) the Psalms, but also that Moses wrote the entirety of the first five books of the Bible (the Pentateuch or Torah), or that Solomon wrote Proverbs, Ecclesiastes, and the Song of Songs, frequently called "The Song of Solomon." Attributions like these are not made entirely willy-nilly but these attributions are also not entirely accurate—not by any means. Early biblical interpreters noted millennia ago that Moses could not have written about his own burial (Deut. 34); various proverbs are attributed to people other than Solomon (see, e.g., Prov. 22:17; 24:23; 30:1; 31:1); and the Song of Songs speaks about Solomon in the third person (1:5; 3:7, 9, 11) and may even poke fun at him (Song 8:11–12). Even if some of these compositions go back to David, Moses, and Solomon (or their times), that doesn't get us any closer to what these compositions *mean*. The meaning is found in what these texts say to us now—*regardless* of who wrote them, where, or when.

In brief, "David wrote the Psalms" and similar historical assertions, especially about authorship and how that impinges on interpretation, are often unhelpful because we cannot determine the accuracy of such assertions with anything approaching certainty and, more to the point, determining their accuracy is largely irrelevant—it may be an exercise in missing the poetic point of the Psalms, the epistolary point of Hebrews, the pedagogical point of Proverbs, and so forth. And to do that would be unhelpful *to the extreme*.

Former U.S. Poet Laureate, Billy Collins, has a poem about teaching poetry in which he says he wants his students to be like water-skiers, skiing on a poem like it was the surface of a lake, waving to people on the shore—in this case the author of the poem, or at least the poet's name. But instead, all his students want to do is take the poem hostage and "torture a confession out of it," beating it to extract the answer of "what it really means."[1] To stay with Collins' imagery, the biblical author (or perhaps the biblical author's name) is present, certainly, whenever we read and interpret Scripture, but it is way *over there*, on the shore. What matters most immediately is the wondrous depth of Scripture that we are waterskiing on! Anything that detracts from that wondrous depth, from Scripture itself, and that would replace Scripture as somehow more determinative and more important than Scripture, is an "unhelpful historical assertion." Again: *To the extreme*.

St. Augustine celebrated the imponderable depths of Scripture:

> The wondrous depth of your utterances, whose surface may indeed be flattering to the childish, but the wondrous depth, my God, the wondrous depth! It gives one a shudder to peer into it—a shudder of awe, and a tremor of love.[2]

Unhelpful historical assertions are, according to Collins' poem, equivalent to torturing Scripture. According to Augustine, such shallow matters are childish dabblings. The ultimate significance of Scripture lies *elsewhere, deeper*.

But, we might ask: Doesn't history matter at all when it comes to the Bible? Of course it does! If nothing else, the Apostles' Creed makes sure we know that Jesus' death took place "under Pontius Pilate," a specific Roman official that we know governed Palestine from 26–36 BCE. But the Creed is about far more than just Pilate or the dates of his rule. Or consider this example: We aren't even sure how old Jesus was when he began his ministry. Of the Gospel writers, only Luke says anything about it, and he offers just a rough guestimate: "Jesus was *about thirty* when he began his work" (Luke 3:23). So, if push ever comes to shove, instead of unhelpful historical assertions like "David wrote the Psalms," we should take our cue from the New Testament authors who say, in the end (or rather from the start), that Scripture goes back, ultimately, to God, speaking by the Holy Spirit.

CLARIFICATION 6:
Historical background information is often important, but is often not nearly as important as people think. Who, exactly, wrote what and when and where is far less important than what, exactly, is written.

QUESTIONS FOR DISCUSSION

1. Have you been led to believe that David wrote (all) the Psalms? If so, have you felt that David's authorship meant that each psalm must be related to his life?
2. Does the attempt to assign authorship to a section of Scripture help or hinder its interpretation? Why do you think some biblical writers suggested that certain Scriptures were written by major figures in the faith (be it Moses, David, Solomon, or Paul)?
3. Does it help you to think about Scripture's ultimate author as God? How do you correlate that kind of

divine authorship with the human authorship of the biblical writings?

4. Besides the question of authorship, what other unhelpful historical assertions are you familiar with when it comes to the interpretation of Scripture? What problems might we encounter if we treat the Bible like "a history book" (see Mistruth 2)?

5. Conversely, what kind of historical assertions are helpful, even necessary, when it comes to the interpretation of Scripture?

THE OLD TESTAMENT
ISN'T SPIRITUALLY ENRICHING

If you're in my line of work, it's hard to take Mistruth 7 seriously. I've devoted my life to studying the Old Testament, so of course I find it eminently spiritually enriching. It is hard, therefore—at least for me—to imagine anyone with the slightest bit of familiarity with the Old Testament not finding it spiritually enriching. In fact, in my judgment, the Old Testament is so spiritually enriching that I couldn't possibly do the topic justice with a very long book let alone with a few pages in a small one. Also, given my line of work, I have to admit that I suspect that Mistruth 7 (and also Mistruth 8, which is related), is in some fashion asserted in comparison to the New Testament. Many people, perhaps because they are unfamiliar with it, don't find the Old Testament as enriching as the New Testament. Whatever the case, let me mention an important starting point for thinking about the Old Testament's spiritual significance before offering a few examples with regard to the spiritual riches it offers us.

The *starting point* is that what we find in the Old Testament depends a lot on what we expect to find. This is to echo some things that were already said in Mistruth 2.

Do we expect to find a boring history book when we read the Old Testament? Then that will probably be what we find—or that expectation may be enough reason to not even crack it open to find anything at all. To return to the work of Ellen Davis, which I cited earlier in this regard (Mistruth 2), do we know *what* to look for and *how to look* for it (patiently, carefully, attentively) so that seeking, we shall find (cf. Matt. 7:7; Luke 11:9)?[1] To put the matter more directly: the Old Testament is spiritually enriching if it is read for spiritual enrichment, if we approach it as a spiritually enriching book, if we come to it expecting to be addressed by a word that can change us for the better. If we do these things, there is hardly a nook or cranny of the Old Testament that *won't* be spiritually enriching in some way, shape, or form.

It is easy enough to think about a famous story like the exodus narrative and how that has served as inspiration for Christians throughout history, not least among African Americans from the time of slavery to the present day. Harriet Tubman, who led people from slavery to freedom on the Underground Railroad, was called "Moses"—and for good reason. Christians who lived centuries before the founding of America and the African slave trade also found the story of redemption mapped onto the book of Exodus. Coming out of Egypt, from under an oppressive Pharaoh, was equivalent to being saved from sin, crossing the Reed Sea (Exodus 15) was like coming through the waters of baptism, and the promised land was the ultimate goal of heaven.

Given the starting point—that *all* of the Old Testament is spiritually enriching—it is not surprising to hear that Christians have found inspiration off the beaten track, not just with famous texts like the exodus narrative. A well-known example is found in the eighty-six sermons that Bernard of Clairvaux (1090–1153 BCE) wrote on the Song of Songs, and he only got through the first verse of chapter 3 in that book! Every word in Scripture—*every single syllable*—was to be savored and considered with reference to the life of faith.

With that starting point in place, and as one possible entrée into the subject, let's consider a few of the themes found in the Apostles' Creed and how they are also found in the Old Testament. Surely themes from the Creed are spiritually enriching for Christians to know, contemplate, and recite! Here, then, is the Creed along with a few of the themes that some of its lines evoke.

The Apostles' Creed	*Themes*
I believe in God, the Father almighty,	
creator of heaven and earth.	*Creation*
I believe in Jesus Christ, his only Son,	
our Lord,	
who was conceived by the	
Holy Spirit	
and born of the virgin Mary.	*Incarnation*
He suffered under Pontius Pilate,	*Suffering*
was crucified, died, and was buried;	
he descended to hell.	
The third day he rose again from	
the dead.	
He ascended to heaven	
and is seated at the right hand of	
God the Father almighty.	
From there he will come to judge	
the living and the dead.	*Judgment*
I believe in the Holy Spirit,	
the holy catholic church,	
the communion of saints,	*The People of God*
the forgiveness of sins,	*Forgiveness*
the resurrection of the body,	
and the life everlasting. Amen.	

Where do the creedal themes listed above show up in the Old Testament? The answer is "all over the place." *Creation* is the subject of the Bible's very first chapter in its very first book. But creation is also discussed in many places outside of Genesis 1: Genesis 2, for example, Psalm 74, Proverbs 8, and elsewhere—including John 1. The Old Testament's testimonies about creation are spiritually enriching by highlighting the radical dependence of *everything*, not just human beings, on the God who created heaven and earth (see Gen. 14:19, 22; 1 Kgs. 19:15; 2 Chr. 2:12) and who cares for all (see Pss. 104; 146:6–9)—so much so that we can, like the psalmists, say that our help comes from that same Lord, "the maker of heaven and earth" (Pss. 121:2; 124:8 CEB). Further, at least one meaning of the "image of God" idea known from the first creation story (Gen. 1:27–28) would be to act like God does in the opening chapters of Genesis: benevolently, nonviolently, creatively, generously, with blessing. To act in such ways would be to be in God's image by imaging God.

Incarnation is a term that is usually associated with Jesus in the New Testament, but the eschatological vision of Revelation 21:3, that "God's dwelling is here with humankind. He will dwell with them, and they will be his peoples. God himself will be with them as their God" (CEB) is a notion found already in the Old Testament, especially in the tabernacle that is discussed extensively in almost mind-numbing detail in Exodus 25–30 (instructions) and again in Exodus 35–40 (construction). In fact, the language of John 1:14, which states that the Word became flesh and "lived" among us (or "made his home among us" CEB) likely depends on language used to refer to the tabernacle, the Tent of Meeting, which the glory of the Lord filled and which accompanied Israel on its journey from Egypt to the promised land. Jesus, John says, "tabernacled" among us just like God did with Israel in the Pentateuch. Beyond the tabernacle, there is the incarnational ministry of the prophets, who bore God's grief in their lives and their work (e.g., Jeremiah), even in their marriages (e.g., Hosea). And then there is Moses, who, in Deuteronomy, suffers vicariously for and because of Israel (Deut. 1:37; 3:26).

Suffering is a major theme, perhaps *the* major theme of the Psalms. The book of Psalms has always been held precious by the church, not only for its hymns of praise (since there are, comparatively speaking, not that many of those), but also because of its laments and prayers for help, which show how deeply the faithful struggle in both life and in faith. The Psalms have drawn the attention of the greatest Christian writers: from St. Augustine, to Martin Luther, to Dietrich Bonhoeffer, to C. S. Lewis, and many, many more. The Psalms are the hymnbook of ancient Israel but also (according to Luther), "a Little Bible," because the Psalter contains everything the Bible contains yet within the much smaller compass of 150 poems full of pain, thanksgiving, and praise, or, to use more recent terminology, the Psalms are full of the three essential prayers: help, thanks, and wow.[2] And what of Job? Has there ever been a more enduring treatment of the problem of righteous suffering than what is found in that book? Those who don't find the book of Job spiritually enriching have likely never read it. Or, if they have, they haven't read it well, perhaps because they are not sufficiently acquainted with suffering to even begin to comprehend it.

God's *judgment* has already been treated in Mistruth 4, where I tried to make the case that the wrath of God is in service to benevolent, even therapeutic ends: that we and our world might be changed for the better. The Creed knows of this "positive" side to judgment as it expresses the expectation and hope ("I believe") in Christ's return to judge "the living and the dead." Even divine judgment, that is, can be spiritually enriching. Divine judgment is also cause for joy in the Psalms, where the hills and the trees of the forest sing for joy because the Lord is coming to judge the earth—the Lord who "will judge the world with righteousness, and the peoples with his truth" (96:12–13; see also 98:8–9).

The Old Testament's focus on *the people of God* is yet another spiritually enriching element. The New Testament, too, speaks of the community of faith, but it is quite common, especially in our modern, highly individualized society, to read the New Testament as mostly a personal affair about "Jesus and me." In fact, some people are so tainted by contemporary individualism that they think social and political matters are not to be mixed with religion—as if they could ever be separated. Even if someone persists in such naiveté with regard to the New Testament (where it is also not justified: Christ, not Caesar, is Lord), the corporate nature of the Old Testament simply cannot be missed. The Old Testament's emphasis is everywhere on Israel *as a group*: first as a family, then a people, and then a nation with land—a nation that stands together in covenant with God, receiving rewards, yes, even punishments, *as a group*. This corporate emphasis is spiritually enriching because it reminds us that the life of faith is never solely a matter of private, individualized piety. Instead, biblical faith is fundamentally and at root a communal matter. It concerns *the polis* as much as it does *the pious*.

As a final creedal theme we can consider *forgiveness*. There are, first and foremost, several famous texts about forgiveness in the Old Testament—Psalm 51, for example, or the first chapter of Isaiah:

> Come now, and let's settle this,
> says the LORD.
> Though your sins are like scarlet,
> they will be white as snow.
> If they are red as crimson,
> they will become like wool.
>
> (Isa. 1:18 CEB)

And then there is the great "manual of sacrifice" found in Leviticus 1–7. Now, granted, this is not likely most Christians' favorite part of the Bible, but the sacrificial system found in Leviticus is of utmost importance, especially coming, as it does, hard on the heels of the book of Exodus, where nearly everything was lost after the worship of the golden calf (see Exodus 32–34). Israel knows, Scripture knows, *God* knows that there must be mechanisms in place to set things right again (see further, Mistruth 9). And that is exactly what happens in the sacrificial system so that the person in question, including "you," can be forgiven—and *is* in fact forgiven (see Lev. 4:20, 26, 31, 35; 5:10, 13, 15, 19; 6:7; 19:22). Of course, the Old Testament knows that "to obey is better than sacrifice" (1 Sam. 15:22) and that there is more to life with God, and to forgiveness from God, than sacrifice alone (see, e.g., Pss. 40:6; 50:7–15, 23; 51:16–17; Isa. 1:11–17; Amos 5:21–24; and Mistruth 3 above).

We shouldn't be surprised in the least that these spiritually enriching themes from the Old Testament resonate with the famous summary of Christian faith known as the Apostles' Creed (and vice versa). Second Timothy 3:16–17 is quite clear that "every scripture" is not only inspired by God, it is also "useful for teaching, for showing mistakes, for correcting, and for training character, so that the person who belongs to God can be equipped to do everything that is good" (CEB). One could hardly imagine a better description of "spiritually enriching" than that. And by "every scripture," you'll recall from Mistruth 1, 2 Timothy means the Old Testament!

CLARIFICATION 7:
The Old Testament is spiritually enriching
in countless profound ways.

QUESTIONS FOR DISCUSSION

1. What is your definition of "spiritually enriching"? Name a text (from anywhere in Scripture) that you think is spiritually enriching and specify why.

2. Have you ever thought of the Old Testament as *not* spiritually enriching? If so, what part(s) and why? Conversely, what parts of the Old Testament have you *always* found spiritually enriching (if any), and why?

3. Regardless of how you answered question 2, can you identify some part of the Old Testament that, on the face of it, does *not* seem spiritually enriching? With fresh eyes and the basic starting point discussed in this chapter, revisit that part of the Bible to see if it might be spiritually nurturing after all. Did you find what you were seeking? Why or why not?

4. Pick one of the creedal themes treated in this chapter and see if you can think of other texts from the Old Testament to round it out even further.

5. Identify a theme from the Apostles' Creed that is not treated in this chapter and trace where it is also found in the Old Testament.

THE OLD TESTAMENT ISN'T PRACTICALLY RELEVANT

Mistruth 8 seems to be closely related to Mistruth 7, and for more than one reason. For one thing, Mistruth 8, like Mistruth 7, may depend on an implicit comparison with the New Testament: "The Old Testament isn't *as* practically relevant *as the New Testament.*" Second, "practically relevant" probably means "spiritually enriching" to lots of people, though these mistruths can be distinguished, even if only for sake of discussion. Mistruth 7 can be seen as theological (pertaining to our beliefs about and faith in God) and Mistruth 8 more about behavior (ethics).

Correcting Mistruth 8 requires proceeding on more than one path because much depends on what "practically relevant" means. So, first, if "practically relevant" really is code for "spiritually enriching," then it is time to reread the chapter on Mistruth 7. If Mistruth 8 means that the Old Testament isn't *useful* (a synonym for "practical") and *pertinent* (a synonym for "relevant") for Christian life and practice, I would have to at least register my life's work as one piece of evidence to the contrary. After all, as a seminary professor, I've devoted my entire life to teaching the Old Testament to people training for Christian ministry.

Then there are countless Christian ministers who have spent innumerable hours studying the Old Testament for the purposes of teaching and preaching. This alone would seem to more than suffice to demonstrate the practical utility and relevant pertinence of the Old Testament to Christian faith and service.

Beyond these examples drawn from the work of various professionals, let me mention three things that show Mistruth 8 is in need of correction.

1. Let's begin with a fuller, comparative form of Mistruth 8, which relates it to the New Testament. What, we might ask, is practically relevant about the New Testament? Much, no doubt, especially if "practically relevant" means "spiritually enriching" (see Mistruth 7). Beyond that, however, perhaps the New Testament's practical relevance is to be found in its many admonitions, in its moral exhortation. This sort of thing is found in "preachy" passages in the Gospels—perhaps above all the Sermon on the Mount in Matthew 5–7 and the Sermon on the Plain in Luke 6:17–49—and in some of the more extended (and explained) parables of Jesus. Maybe even more representative is the way Paul typically ends his letters with exhortations of various sorts. Here's a short example from Philippians, lined out to get a sense of how many instructions Paul can pack into a very short space:

Rejoice in the Lord always;
again I will say, Rejoice.
Let your gentleness be known to everyone. The Lord
is near.
Do not worry about anything,
but in everything by prayer and supplication with
thanksgiving let your requests be made known to
God. And the peace of God, which surpasses all
understanding, will guard your hearts and your
minds in Christ Jesus.

Finally, beloved, whatever is true, whatever is
    honorable, whatever is just, whatever is pure,
    whatever is pleasing, whatever is commendable,
    if there is any excellence and if there is anything
    worthy of praise, think about these things.
Keep on doing the things that you have learned and
    received and heard and seen in me, and the God of
    peace will be with you.

(Phil. 4:4–9)

Here's another from Colossians:

Devote yourselves to prayer,
keeping alert in it with thanksgiving.
At the same time pray for us as well that God will open
    to us a door for the word, that we may declare the
    mystery of Christ, for which I am in prison, so that
    I may reveal it clearly, as I should.
Conduct yourselves wisely toward outsiders, making
    the most of the time.
Let your speech always be gracious, seasoned with
    salt, so that you may know how you ought to
    answer everyone.

(Col. 4:2–6)

And one last, chockfull, example from 1 Thessalonians:

But we appeal to you, brothers and sisters, to
    respect those who labor among you, and have
    charge of you in the Lord and admonish you;
esteem them very highly in love because of their work.
Be at peace among yourselves.
And we urge you, beloved, to admonish the idlers,
encourage the fainthearted,
help the weak,
be patient with all of them.

See that none of you repays evil for evil,
but always seek to do good to one another and
    to all.
Rejoice always,
pray without ceasing,
give thanks in all circumstances; for this is the will
    of God in Christ Jesus for you.
Do not quench the Spirit.
Do not despise the words of prophets,
but test everything;
hold fast to what is good;
abstain from every form of evil.

(1 Thess. 5:12–22)

Since this sort of thing is all over the epistles, many more examples could be offered, including from the non-Pauline letters, especially James, but the point is clear: the Epistles are full of injunctions—commands even—that seem *uber* practically relevant.

True enough, and good, too! That said, it has to be admitted that passages like these start blurring together after a while—not just amongst themselves, but even within themselves. It's a bit hard, that is, to keep straight that list of seventeen different things to do in 1 Thessalonians, especially because there are still other things 1 Thessalonians wants us to do. Not to mention 2 Thessalonians and all the rest. Practically relevant? Sure, if that means "having to do with everyday life," but that doesn't mean it's easy—not easy to keep straight and even less easy to do. This first item, then, is just that "practically relevant" doesn't mean "easily done."

2. The second item is that if practical relevance can be linked with passages like the ones I've cited from Paul's letters, well, then, the Old Testament is *full* of practical relevance just like that. The Old Testament contains not one, not two, but three types of literature that come across a lot like these passages from the Epistles: the

first is *law*, the second is *prophecy*, and the third is *wisdom*. I cover Old Testament *law* and some of its practical relevance in Mistruth 9 (see below). Even so, think of the practical relevance to be found in the Ten Commandments (Exod. 20), or in Leviticus 19 (discussed in Mistruth 5). Consider just a few of the ethical instructions in Leviticus 19:

> You shall be holy, for I the LORD your God am holy. (v. 2)
>
> You shall each revere your mother and father. (v. 3a)
>
> You shall not steal; you shall not deal falsely; and you shall not lie to one another. (v. 11)
>
> You shall not revile the deaf or put a stumbling block before the blind. (v. 14a)
>
> You shall not render an unjust judgment; you shall not be partial to the poor or defer to the great; with justice you shall judge your neighbor. (v. 15)
>
> You shall not hate in your heart anyone of your kin. (v. 17a)
>
> You shall not take vengeance or bear a grudge against any of your people. (v. 18a)

Even these few, highly practical commandments would be enough to create a kind, generous, and just society — or at least a kind, generous, and just community of faith!

I've talked a bit about *prophecy* already in Mistruth 4, where I noted that the Prophets urge their audiences to change their behavior (repent) by living lives free of injustice and sin. Such preaching, which is profoundly ethical, is also — and as a result — profoundly "practically relevant." One example from a cast of thousands:

> Seek good and not evil,
> that you may live;

And so the LORD, the God of hosts, will be
   with you,
just as you have said.
Hate evil and love good,
   and establish justice in the gate.
                              (Amos 5:14–15a)

Wisdom literature may be the most obviously practical
of these three genres, however, since it has to do with wise
living in the world. The Old Testament books of wisdom
are typically identified as Proverbs, Job, Ecclesiastes,
and (sometimes) the Song of Songs. The Song of Songs
is a collection of love poems celebrating the love of a man
(not Solomon—see Mistruth 6) and a woman—it may
well be practically relevant on the ways of romance but
it admittedly doesn't venture much beyond that subject.
Those two kids are too much in love to talk about anything else. Job is an extended treatment of the problem
of righteous suffering (see Mistruth 7). As such, it is a bit
heady, more theoretical and abstract, perhaps, than the
conclusions of Paul's letters. Maybe Job is closer to
the meat of Paul's letters, especially something dense like
the Epistle to the Romans. As such, Job may be quite relevant, but in ways that are more intellectual than practical.
Then again, much can be gained practically by watching the friends and what they do, mostly because they
fail rather miserably when it comes to offering pastoral
care to Job. They start out strong, mostly by sitting with
Job and keeping their big mouths shut (2:13), but then
they get involved in a protracted theoretical debate with
Job that mostly just beats up on the poor guy while he's
down. No wonder Job calls them "worthless physicians"
(13:4) and no surprise when God tells them that they
haven't spoken rightly, as Job has (42:7–8). Note to self:
Don't engage in theological debate in the ICU or at the
morgue!

That leaves Proverbs and Ecclesiastes, which are *full* of practical advice about all sorts of things. Proverbs alone contains more than 370 maxims about life and wise living in chapters 10–22 alone. Talk about not easy to keep straight and also not easily done! And yet, as true as that may be, it is equally true that the book of Proverbs is the proverbial gold mine of good advice that is eminently useful and apparently timeless. Here are a few nuggets excavated almost at random:

> Hatred stirs up strife, but love covers all offenses. (10:12)
>
> Whoever belittles another lacks sense, but an intelligent person remains silent. (11:12)
>
> Rash words are like sword thrusts, but the tongue of the wise brings healing. (12:18)
>
> A soft answer turns away wrath, but a harsh word stirs up anger. (15:1)
>
> Better is a dinner of vegetables where love is than a fatted ox and hatred with it. (15:17)

And so on and so forth, and *extensively*! The book of Ecclesiastes is more of the same but with a twist: that book is far more skeptical than Proverbs is about how the world works and what human beings, finally, can know about all of that with certainty (the answer Ecclesiastes offers to that last question is "very little"). Even so, Ecclesiastes, too, is full of practical wisdom. Here is a very brief and non-representative sampler:

> Never be rash with your mouth, nor let your heart be quick to utter a word before God, for God is in heaven, and you upon earth; therefore let your words be few. (5:2)

When you make a vow to God, do not delay fulfilling it; for he has no pleasure in fools. Fulfill what you vow. It is better that you should not vow than that you should vow and not fulfill it. (5:4–5)

Do not say, "Why were the former days better than these?" For it is not from wisdom that you ask this. (7:10)

To summarize this second point, the Old Testament, no less than the New, is full of material that speaks directly to everyday ethical activity. In fact, given the length of the Old Testament compared to the New, the range of topics covered by the Old Testament is far vaster than what we find in the New Testament. In terms of sheer quantity, that is, the Old Testament is *far more* practically relevant than the New.

One quick additional point: the wisdom literature of the Old Testament doesn't just *talk about* the wise life, informing us about it. No, it wants—and is designed—to *cultivate* the wise life, which makes this material even more practically relevant. Consider the following passage from Proverbs:

Do not answer fools according to their folly, or you will be a fool yourself.
Answer fools according to their folly, or they will be wise in their own eyes.
(26:4–5)

A conundrum if ever there was one: two verses right next to each other commending, or rather commanding, contrary advice. What is one to do? Which verse is the one to be followed? The answer of course is "yes," meaning, of course, *both*! Both maxims are right but not at the exact same time. The wise person must know which one to use when. They must also know how to use each one. The wise person will know which to use and when (and how) because the wise person has prudence, *practical wisdom*, that helps one know what to do and when to do it. What could be more practical than that? And as for relevance, Proverbs 15:23 could stand as a summary of wise speech (if not also prudence more generally):

> To give an appropriate answer is a joy;
> how good is a word at the right time!
> (CEB)

3. My third and final item is to sound a cautionary note. In my experience, the attempt to find "practical relevance" in the Bible is sometimes due to a type of reading that is too hurried and too utilitarian. I've already noted earlier in this book that the best reading of Scripture is marked by virtues like patience and careful attention to what is there (see Mistruths 2 and 7). I worry, therefore, that our interest in finding something "practically relevant" in the Bible may sometimes lead us to miss what Scripture actually has for us.

The great theologian and martyr, Dietrich Bonhoeffer, issued a similar warning in a lecture given on August 23, 1935, in his underground and illegal seminary in Nazi Germany. In this lecture, Bonhoeffer worried about the tendency among many Christians to contemporize the New Testament—to make it relevant, that is, for today.[1] Bonhoeffer thought that that was a terrible idea because it made us and our time the arbiter of what was important in the New Testament. Instead of doing that, he said, what Christians should do is take themselves and their contemporary context and judge that by the proper subject matter of the New Testament (God's work in Christ). *That* is the proper order: the New Testament judges us today. The reverse, improper order—the attempt to make the New

Testament "contemporary"—was equivalent, in his opinion, to paganism.[2]

I have to admit that, ever since I first read that essay, I have studiously avoided the word "relevant" whenever it comes to the Bible.

CLARIFICATION 8:
The Old Testament is useful for Christian practice in a whole host of ways, on a whole host of topics, and from a whole host of sources.

QUESTIONS FOR DISCUSSION:

1. How do you define "practically relevant"?
2. Where do you find the most practically relevant material in the Old Testament? New Testament? Are there certain genres, books, or passages that stand out?
3. Can you find examples like the ones from Proverbs or Paul's letters used in this chapter elsewhere in the Old and New Testaments? How are the passages you found practically relevant?
3. After reading this chapter, do you agree that texts like Proverbs or the Prophets or the Pentateuch are practically relevant? Why or why not?
3. What dangers might there be in letting our reading of Scripture be driven overmuch by our own concerns with what is "relevant" to the contemporary moment?

THE OLD TESTAMENT LAW IS NOTHING BUT A BURDEN, IMPOSSIBLE TO KEEP

Many years ago, I was at an ice-skating rink during the holidays with a range of extended family. As I carefully made my way around the oval (I am not a good skater), the conversation with one of my in-laws turned — as it so often does — to theology and, even better, to the Bible and the Old Testament.

I don't remember all the details now but, not unlike the exchange with Tom described in Mistruth 1, the conversation turned to the significance of the Old Testament, its relationship to the New Testament, and so forth. All easy topics! As part of this, the Old Testament Law somehow came up, and Jesus, and the relationship of those two (if not also of Christianity and Judaism) — again, easy topics to cover in one, maybe at most two, circuits around the rink! While the full discussion is fuzzy, I do remember my in-law turning to me with a genuine and earnest query:

"I thought," she said, "Jesus came because we couldn't keep the law."

"I think," I replied, "Jesus came because we didn't keep it."

The difference in those two sentences is slight, grammatically, but truly massive, theologically. My in-law thought the necessity of Jesus' incarnation was related to the inability of people to keep the Old Testament Law: at best the Law was a burden they couldn't, in the end, shoulder. My response (and, again, I have to admit that perhaps it was a bit quick) suggested Jesus' incarnation was necessary not because humans were incapable of keeping the law but because human beings simply didn't keep it—*wouldn't* keep it might even be a better way of putting it.

The reason for Christ's incarnation is most definitely *not* an easy topic and would require many times around the ice-skating rink. My family member's remark is nevertheless instructive because it shows how Mistruth 9, that the Old Testament Law is nothing but a burden, impossible to keep, is connected (as so many of the mistruths are) to opinions Christians have about the New Testament and Jesus and how all of that is related.

The relationship of Jesus, Paul, and the New Testament as a whole to Old Testament Law is also too big to discuss here, but we would all do well to remember Matthew 5:17–20, which I cited earlier (Mistruth 3):

> "Do not think that I have come to abolish the law or the prophets; I have come not to abolish but to fulfill. For truly I tell you, until heaven and earth pass away, not one letter, not one stroke of a letter, will pass from the law until all is accomplished. Therefore, whoever breaks one of the least of these commandments, and teaches others to do the same, will be called least in the kingdom of heaven; but whoever does them and teaches them will be called great in the kingdom of heaven. For I tell you, unless your righteousness exceeds that of the scribes and Pharisees, you will never enter the kingdom of heaven."

With Jesus' words in Matthew duly entered, let's look more closely at the Old Testament proper to correct Mistruth 9.

1. Before proceeding any further, "Old Testament Law" should probably be defined. It is generally understood to be the first five books of the Old Testament, called the Pentateuch, or Torah, which means "law" or "instruction" in Hebrew. There is much more than legal prescriptions in the Pentateuch, however. There are stories and poems in addition to the 613 laws that the rabbis delineated in the Torah. Whatever the case, when people speak of Old Testament Law today, they are generally referring to the legal materials in the Pentateuch, which are found primarily in Exodus through Deuteronomy. These laws concern everything from proper diet to care for the poor, respect for elders, building construction, sacrifice, agriculture, care of animals, crime and punishment, property, and so on and so forth. Old Testament Law is a truly capacious category and includes the Ten Commandments (Exod. 20:1–17 and Deut. 5:6–21) along with several distinct and identifiable collections like the "Book of the Covenant" (Exod. 20:22–23:33), the Priestly Law (Exod. 25–Num. 36), and the Deuteronomic Law (Deut. 12–26).

2. With that working definition in place, some of the implications of Mistruth 9 can be explored further. One of these is that, if the Old Testament Law is only a burden, and truly impossible to keep as well, there must be some sort of fatal flaw in it. The problem with such a reasonable deduction is that the flaw that is thus posited would have to trace back further, not stopping at the Law itself, but extending all the way back to the *Lawgiver*. In the Old Testament, of course, it is none other than God who gives the Law to Israel. It seems unfair, to say the very least, of God to impose a burden on God's people—something that God knows full well is impossible to keep. In point of fact, the Pentateuch *never* presents the Law as something designed

to frustrate the people; quite to the contrary, it is part of the covenant relationship that Israel willingly enters into in grateful response to the prior gracious salvation of God, experienced in the exodus from Egypt.

Let me repeat that because it is important: God's gracious action toward Israel in the exodus from Egypt *happens first, before* the Law is given at Sinai. Grace comes first, and only then covenantal obedience—*even in the Old Testament!* If Christians remembered only this point—a point that is obvious from even a surface reading of the book of Exodus—it would go a long way to correcting some serious misconceptions Christians often have about the Old Testament and Judaism. In a word: there is no "works righteousness" in the Old Testament or Judaism. The Law is thus a measure of grateful obedience offered back to a gracious God. In this way the Law is a means—a *divinely given* means—to maintain the relationship with the Lord who saves. Not surprisingly, then, upon arriving at Mount Sinai, Israel is given the choice to enter into what is a reciprocal covenant or to refuse that invitation (Exod. 19:3–6). The response Israel offers is unequivocal: "Everything that the LORD has spoken we will do" (Exod. 19:8).

Now, in fairness, that response is right out of the gate—from the get-go—before Israel has heard much of anything and very little Law proper. The first laws Israel hears as part of the covenant are the Ten Commandments and that is plenty! Israel has heard enough: the Israelites fear for their lives because this covenant is serious business and the Lord of the covenant is not to be trifled with. After the Ten, the Israelites ask Moses to serve as intermediary for the rest of the Lord's Law (Exod. 19:18–21).

But, again, despite the needed intercession by Moses, the Law is never presented as a frustrating impossibility, as nothing but a burden. Instead, as Psalm 1 puts it, the Lord's Law was seen as a source of delight, worthy of mediating on day and night (Ps. 1:2). Psalm 19 goes further: the Law of the Lord is perfect, sure, right, clear, pure, true, more desirable than gold, sweeter than honey (Ps. 19:7–10). Psalm 119, the longest of all the Psalms, goes even further, devoting 176 verses to praising the Law of God. "Oh, how I love your law!" the poet of Psalm 119 sings (v. 97). "I've seen that everything, no matter how perfect, has a limit, but your commandment is boundless," the psalmist asserts (v. 96 CEB). "I will never forget your precepts, for by them you have given me life" (v. 93) is this psalmist's personal testimony. None of this comes remotely near any idea that the Law (let alone the God who gave the Law) is flawed in some fatal, foundational way. Quite to the contrary—and there's still 173 more verses in Psalm 119 that could be cited on the point.

3. There's still more testimony to consider; let's call this *the testimony of the faithful*. Proceeding in canonical order we can begin with the picture of perfectly obedient Israel in Exodus 35–40. The picture prior to these chapters is a much different story. Indeed, right after getting the Ten Commandments, especially the first two about no other gods and no idols, we read about the golden calf debacle (let's call it "Calfgate" for now) where Israel breaks both of those crucial commandments at the very moment of covenant-making (Exod. 32). It's the religious equivalent of committing adultery on one's wedding night. Just when all seems lost, however, thanks to some savvy intercession by Moses, all is not lost and Israel finds itself reinstated and forgiven by "the LORD, a God merciful and gracious, slow to anger, and abounding in steadfast love and faithfulness, keeping steadfast love for the thousandth generation, forgiving iniquity and transgression and sin" (Exod. 34:6–7a). After the renewal of the covenant (including a new set of tablets and commandments; see Exod. 34), Israel is ready and willing, able and empowered to carry out the instructions about the tabernacle that were given in Exodus 25–30. And so they do—to a T! Even after the

gravest of disobedience, that is, Exodus 35–40 shows that things can be set right and the freshly forgiven can find themselves perfectly obedient, "just as" God commanded (Exod. 39:32, 42–43).

Next up is Moses. In his valedictory speech to Israel in Deuteronomy, at the very end, after the great number of laws found in chapters 12–26, Moses offers this encouraging word:

> This commandment that I'm giving you right now is definitely not too difficult for you. It isn't unreachable. It isn't up in heaven somewhere so that you have to ask, "Who will go up for us to heaven and get it for us that we can hear it and do it?" Nor is it across the ocean somewhere so that you have to ask, "Who will cross the ocean for us and get it for us that we can hear it and do it?" Not at all! The word is very close to you. It's in your mouth and in your heart, waiting for you to do it. (Deut. 30:11–14 CEB)

Not unreachable, not too difficult, not too far. Instead: very close, in the mouth and heart, ready to be enacted. Exodus 35–40 already proved Moses right!

Then there's that man from the land of Uz named Job, who "was blameless and upright, one who feared God and turned away from evil" (Job 1:1). "Nobody's *that* perfect," we might retort but if we keep reading, we see that this judgment isn't limited to the anonymous narrator of the book of Job. *Even God* recognizes Job's perfection, not once but twice (1:8; 2:3). In fact, if Job isn't *that* perfect, the book of Job flounders—the entire composition hinges, at least in the first two chapters, on Job's amazing, dare one say *flawless*, religiosity.

If we think this kind of testimony is limited to the Old Testament, we should think again. There are Jesus' words in Matthew 5:17–20 to reckon with, especially the admonition in verse 20 that the righteousness of Jesus' followers must *exceed* that of the scribes and Pharisees. Paul, too—yes, *even* Paul, who frequently says strong things *against* "the law"—has quite a record when it comes to the Law:

> If anyone else has reason to be confident in the flesh, I have more: circumcised on the eighth day, a member of the people of Israel, of the tribe of Benjamin, a Hebrew born of Hebrews; as to the law, a Pharisee; as to zeal, a persecutor of the church; as to righteousness under the law, blameless. (Phil. 3:4b–6)

Did he just say *blameless*? Why, yes, I believe he did.[1]

4. The testimony of these faithful folks is weighty to be sure, but we know, from Scripture if not also from our own track records (and in truth from *both*) that it is easy enough to prove *un*faithful when it comes to God's instruction. If the Law isn't impossible to keep, it is at least highly challenging. But no worries, Old Testament Law contains within itself *provisions for failure*. As I noted in Mistruth 7, the details about sacrifice, including sacrifice for sin, come in Leviticus 1–7, hard and fast on the heels of "Calfgate" in Exodus, showing the way Old Testament Law accounts for, and atones for, disobedience. And the very center of Leviticus, itself the very center of the Torah, is Leviticus 16 which concerns the Day of Atonement, Yom Kippur, when everyone gets all of their sins, of whatever sort or severity, forgiven for sure at least once each year. Yom Kippur and the sacrificial system are all part of Old Testament Law, the Law that God gave. If the Law is a burden, it is a burden that the Law itself helps to carry.

So, whenever we look at the Torah and say "We are terrible at keeping you," the Torah (personified for a moment) looks back at us and says, "Tell me something I don't already know!" And then adds quickly, "But don't worry: I've got it covered." Why the Torah has it covered is not due to some fatal flaw in the Law or the Lawgiver — quite to the contrary! Far from containing some fatal flaw, the Torah's built-in provisions for failure show that the Old Testament Law is not a burden but quite the opposite — a gift — thanks to a genius design feature put there, according to the Old Testament's own witness, by none other than the genius Divine Lawgiver.

What the above considerations indicate is that we should never look at the Torah and say, "We can't keep you." Moses knows better, as did Job (and Job's God), Jesus, and Paul. *Don't keep* or *won't keep* are quite different, at the end of the day, than *can't*. Whatever the grammar, the Old Testament Law and the Lawgiver have already got it covered.

CLARIFICATION 9:
The Old Testament Law is not impossible to keep; the Law is crucial because it is a primary means by which a right relationship with God, fellow humans, the earth, and its creatures is maintained.

QUESTIONS FOR DISCUSSION:

1. Have you ever thought that biblical Law was impossible to keep? Why or why not?
2. After reading this chapter, do you feel differently about the significance of Old Testament Law?
3. How do the testimonies of the faithful affect your understanding of biblical Law?
4. What do you make of the built-in provisions for failure that are found within Old Testament Law? How do these provisions change, if at all, your sense of the purpose, function, and (grace-full) nature of the Law?

5. In light of the biblical sequence that begins with God's grace toward Israel and then moves to Israel's grateful response, how would you now characterize Old Testament Law or any ethical requirements that are found in Scripture?

WHAT REALLY MATTERS IS THAT "EVERYTHING IS ABOUT JESUS"

If several of the previous mistruths have been hard to address, let alone correct (some more than others), Mistruth 10 is probably the trickiest of them all. It seems I've saved the most complicated for last. Mistruth 10 is likely also the most controversial of the ten because many wouldn't deem the statement "everything is about Jesus" to be a mistruth in the least—quite to the contrary, in fact. But if we assume—if only for sake of argument and the duration of this chapter—that Mistruth 10 really *is* a case of misinformation, we might begin by investigating where it came from, where we learned it, and who taught it to us.

According to the title of this book, the answer to the last question is that a preacher (or teacher of some sort) taught it to us, but where did the preacher get it? Perhaps the preacher learned it from someone else—a preacher (or teacher) further up in the supply chain—but there can be no doubt whatsoever that the sentiment, "everything is about Jesus" (or something quite like it) can be found in the pages of the New Testament itself. Probably the most famous passage in this regard is found in Luke 24, the story about the two disciples walking to Emmaus after the crucifixion and resurrection, though they don't seem to believe that last bit quite yet. Suddenly, they are joined by a third traveler, who is Jesus, apparently in disguise since they don't recognize him (vv. 13–16). Jesus, always up for a teaching moment, asks the two what's going on. They can't believe he hasn't heard the news about the crucifixion (his own!) and they also relay the women's report about the resurrection. Jesus interrupts them at just that moment—and not exactly gently:

> Then he said to them, "Oh, how foolish you are, and how slow of heart to believe all that the prophets have declared! Was it not necessary that the Messiah should suffer these things and then enter into his glory?" Then beginning with Moses and all the prophets, he interpreted to them the things about himself in all the scriptures. (Luke 24:25–27)

The key sentence is obviously the last one (v. 27) but the previous one—about the necessity of the Messiah's suffering and glorification (v. 26)—is closely connected. Doesn't this passage, maybe even verse 27 all by itself, *prove* that, when it comes to the Old Testament, "everything really is about Jesus"?

That is what many people have thought, but I'm not fully convinced, for several reasons.

As we've seen earlier in this book (especially in Mistruth 3), while the New Testament sometimes seems to say that the Old Testament has been superseded in one way or another, there's quite a lot in the New Testament that suggests the exact opposite: that the Old Testament remains vital, indispensable, irreplaceable. Matthew 5:17–20 comes to mind, again (see Mistruths 3 and 9), but what about another fascinating story found in Luke, the same Gospel that recounts the road to Emmaus? In Luke 16:19–31, Jesus tells the parable of the rich man and Lazarus.

After their respective deaths, Lazarus is in glory, with Abraham, but the rich man is . . . well, on the other side of a great chasm. But since he's rich (or at least *was* rich), he's a bit entitled and used to getting what he wants. He would really like that poor beggar Lazarus to come take care of his need for a cool drink, since where he finds himself is a bit on the hot side. "Not possible," Abraham says (it's kind of nice to have a heavyweight like him on your team and doing the talking—especially when your opponent is rich and entitled). The rich man then takes a different tack, this one a bit more altruistic. "Just send Lazarus to warn my family so they don't end up here, with me, in this place of torment," he asks. Then things get really interesting:

> Abraham replied, "They have Moses and the Prophets. They must listen to them."
> The rich man said, "No, Father Abraham! But if someone from the dead goes to them, they will change their hearts and lives."
> Abraham said, "If they don't listen to Moses and the Prophets, then neither will they be persuaded if someone rises from the dead." (Luke 16:29–31 CEB)

Once again, the key sentence is obviously the last one (v. 31), but the earlier one—about the necessity of listening to Moses and the prophets (v. 29)—is closely connected. So, then, in this parable, Jesus is crystal clear that Moses and the Prophets are plenty sufficient to avoid the hot place on the wrong side of the chasm. And, if people don't listen to Moses and the Prophets . . . well, not even someone raised from the dead could change their minds, Jesus says in the parable. In the Gospel of Luke, the only person that comes back from the dead after this parable is Jesus himself,[1] and so capital "R" Resurrection seems to be what is at issue. Capital "R" Resurrection won't convince anybody, says the parable, if they aren't already convinced by Moses and the Prophets. Moses and the Prophets are enough—that's what Luke 16 says—though we have to admit that some people, maybe even many, especially those of the rich and entitled variety, will continue to refuse to listen to them.

We could next flip from Luke 16 to the Gospel of John, where Jesus gets into an argument with some people after healing a man on the Sabbath. At the end of the argument, which is really a one-sided lecture by Jesus, he concludes with the following:

> "You search the scriptures because you think that in them you have eternal life; and it is they that testify on my behalf. Yet you refuse to come to me to have life. I do not accept glory from human beings. But I know that you do not have the love of God in you. I have come in my Father's name, and you do not accept me; if another comes in his own name, you will accept him. How can you believe when you accept glory from one another and do not seek the glory that comes from the one who alone is God? Do not think that I will accuse you before the Father; your accuser is Moses, on whom you have set your hope. If you believed Moses, you would believe me, for he wrote about me. But if you do not believe what he wrote, how will you believe what I say? (John 5:39–47)

There is a lot going on in this passage but for present purposes it suffices to observe that the sentiment here seems to be something of a mixture of what is found in Luke 16 and Luke 24. On the one hand, the Scriptures "testify on my [Christ's] behalf" and "he [Moses] wrote about me"—that would be the Luke-24 part of John 5. On the other hand, the connection between Moses and Jesus is a deep, fundamental one: believing Moses leads, apparently automatically, to belief in Jesus (v. 46), and so if you don't already believe in Moses, you can't (or is it won't?) believe in what Jesus says (v. 47)—that's the Luke-16 side of John 5.

More could be said about all this but, for sake of time, let's call it a stalemate for now: some texts in the New Testament appear to suggest not only the necessity but the sufficiency of the Old Testament *all by itself*—that's no real surprise, since the earliest Christians were all Jews and the Old Testament was their Scripture (see Mistruth 1). But other texts from the New Testament seem to indicate that the Old Testament is not sufficient all by itself, or at least that its sufficiency depends on how it relates to and points to Jesus.

When you consider this stalemate in the terms of Mistruth 10, we'd have to say that "everything" may not be about Jesus *only*, but that "everything" cannot *not* be about him (forgive the double negative, but the point is clear). Put differently: what "everything is about" for Christians *must include Jesus* but evidently "everything is about" *more than just Jesus*, even for Christians. Could it be? And what would that *more* be? The Gospel of John offers a not-so-subtle clue: "The Father and I are one," Jesus says (John 10:30). A bit later in the Fourth Gospel, Philip asks Jesus to show him and his fellow disciples the Father, to which Jesus replies:

> "Have I been with you all this time, Philip, and you still do not know me? Whoever has seen me has seen the Father. . . . Do you not believe that I am in the Father and the Father is in me? . . . Believe me that I am in the Father and the Father is in me." (14:8–11a)

And only slightly later Jesus prays to God that the disciples "may be one, as we are one" (17:11) and that the disciples may "be in us" just as "you, Father, are in me and I am in you" (17:21).

What these passages from John suggest is that an approach to the Old Testament's relationship to Jesus need not and should not be restricted to Jesus alone. No, at the very least it must also include *Jesus' Father*, who created the world, saved Israel from Egypt, and gave the Law. And, within the full counsel offered by Christian Trinitarian theology, it must also include the *Holy Spirit*. A Trinitarian reading of the Old Testament—a reading focused on the Triune God—makes sense in a way that a Christological reading—one focused only on Jesus Christ, the second member of the Trinity—simply does not. "Everything is about Jesus" is a mistruth, that is, because of orthodox Trinitarian theology, which asserts that the three members of the Trinity are nevertheless one (see Mistruth 4). In fact, the development and history of Christian theology demonstrates that any inordinate focus on just one member, at the expense of the others, isn't just a bad idea, it's heretical. This is true for the heresy called Monarchianism, which held that only the first member of the Trinity was truly divine. Monarchianism is one form of another type of heresy known as Modalism, in which there is only one God who appears in three different manners or "modes," rather than as three persons.

The Trinity is obviously a complex theological topic—*far more* complicated than metaphors like those saying the Trinity is like an egg (shell, white, yolk) or like H_2O in different forms (ice, water, steam). If things were that simple, it wouldn't have taken a few centuries for the church to work out a robust Trinitarian theology. The point, regardless, is that, while there are definitely three members of the Trinity, no one member is to be favored over the others—to do that is to fall into serious error. The Three are One, in the doctrinal affirmation, but the One are also Three. To focus only on Jesus, to the exclusion of the other members, is thus a grave theological mistake—moreover, it is doctrinal heresy! "Everything is about Jesus" is, therefore, a mistruth because the Trinity is about more than Jesus. "Everything is about the Triune God" is thus a far, far better statement—orthodox, too, and also more accurate for two reasons.

1. The first is that much of the Old Testament is simply not about Jesus—at least not obviously. Take the famous passage in Genesis 3 where God curses the serpent to a life crawling in the dust, adding that:

> I will put enmity between you and the woman, and between your offspring and hers; he will strike your head, and you will strike his heel. (Gen. 3:15)

Is this about Jesus? Well, no, not really—not within the immediate literary context of the story in Genesis—but that has not stopped many people from thinking so. In fact, this passage is sometimes called the *protoevangelium*, the proto- or first-Gospel, because people have seen in the passage something more than the immediate literary context itself. What if the serpent is not just a snake but *something more*: the devil in disguise, perhaps? And what if "the offspring" (note the singular form) of Eve is, ultimately, Jesus Christ? It would make sense that Jesus and the devil are at odds (enmity) with each other. And surely the devil struck at Jesus' heel in the crucifixion but ultimately Jesus crushed the devil's head by defeating death and hell. Viewed in this manner, Genesis 3:15 can be seen as a kind of messianic prophecy. And that is exactly how it was seen by many early church writers with similar interpretations continuing up to the present day.

2. I don't want to say all of that is completely wrong, only that it isn't completely obvious and maybe not

obvious at all, unless, that is, you know about Jesus, you live on this side of the New Testament, and you believe that Jesus is not just a first-century Jew from Nazareth but also the incarnate Son of God, the second member of the eternal Godhead. Even readings that would want to say that "everything" in Genesis 3:15 "is all about Jesus," that is, are dependent, ultimately, on the larger perspective of Christian theology that is fundamentally Trinitarian, which means a larger perspective that is *not* focused solely on Christ. Said differently: if all we care about in the Old Testament is its messianic prophecies, we are not putting it to good use.

According to some biblical scholars, there may be as many as thirty-nine messianic prophecies in the Old Testament—not bad, I guess, but then again that's an average of only one per book.[2] And not even all of those map onto what we find in the New Testament's portrayal of Jesus and his messiahship. Still further, even those Old Testament texts that are taken up in the New Testament and applied to Christ still retain a significance within their original contexts. A famous example is the Immanuel prophecy in Isaiah 7:14, which is cited in Matthew 1:22–23:

> All this took place to fulfill what had been spoken by the Lord through the prophet: "Look, the virgin shall conceive and bear a son, and they shall name him Emmanuel," which means, "God is with us."

In Isaiah 7, however, verse 14 is just one part of a larger unit where God is assuring King Ahaz that the kings who are at his door, threatening Jerusalem, will not succeed. The prophetic word rings a bit hollow—not exactly an answer "at the right time" (Prov. 15:23; see Mistruth 8) if Isaiah is talking only of Jesus who won't be born for seven more centuries.

"Don't worry about a thing, Ahaz: seven hundred years from now everything will be a-okay!"

"Gee, Isaiah, thanks . . . I guess. So what do I do about the armies at the gate?"

God's word to Ahaz through Isaiah must have an imminent referent, an immediate payoff, or it is completely nonsensical. Later, "in the fullness of time" (see Gal. 4:4), that prophetic oracle comes to have even more meaning than it did in eighth-century BCE Jerusalem. And yet, that "more" in no way negates what the oracle meant in Isaiah's time.

In brief, we need to get our money's worth out of the Old Testament. We can't focus only on a handful of messianic prophecies, neglecting, in the process, how even these texts typically have more to say than just what they say about the Messiah. The Old Testament has far more in it than just that. The Old Testament is also obviously and almost everywhere about *God*. Why, then, focus only on Jesus Christ, who never appears explicitly in the Old Testament?

The answer to that last question is probably because we are called "Christians," though that name wasn't coined until a good stretch of time *after* people started following Jesus (Acts 11:26). Regardless, the simple fact is "Christians" don't believe *only* in Jesus. If they did, they would be missing how Jesus and the Father are one (John) and neglecting the giving of the Spirit at Pentecost (Acts 2). In a word, they would be Modalists. Instead, Christians believe in the Triune God and, as noted already in Mistruth 4, Trinitarian theology holds that where one member is present, so are the other two also. When one acts, so also do the other two. They operate *inseparably*.

To sum up: Focusing only on Jesus when it comes to reading the Old Testament, or the whole Bible for that matter —*even when we are reading it explicitly as Christians*— is to inexpertly and inaccurately divide what ultimately cannot be divided, and certainly not simplistically: the Triune God. To assert that "Everything is about Jesus" is to neglect God the Father as well as God the Spirit. Christological or Christocentric readings of the Old Testament (or New for that matter) no doubt mean well. In their own way they are attempts to read the Old Testament (and New) in a Christian way that makes the material spiritually enriching and practically relevant for Christians. But these types of readings are, at the end of the day, misguided if they are the only type of reading we engage in. After all, the Old Testament is *already* spiritually enriching and practically relevant (Mistruths 7–8) and the Old Testament is almost everywhere and always *about God*, almost never explicitly about Jesus Christ.

What that means is that you don't have to assert that "everything is about Jesus"—certainly not Jesus alone—to engage in Christian reading of the Old Testament because wherever the Bible speaks about God, Christian theology asserts that Jesus is there too, as is also the Holy Spirit. We simply don't have to strain and struggle to find Jesus under every rock or behind every "heel" in the Old Testament. Christological or Christocentric readings simply are not necessary—indeed, they may be quite wrong if they are overstated as "everything," as the only kind of Christian approach. *At one and the same time*, however, Trinitarian theology allows us to see every text about God as also relating to Christ and the Spirit (and vice versa). Put differently, reading the Old Testament as Christians does not *require* us to see everything as related to Jesus, even though Christian reading of the Old Testament *allows* us to see everything related to Jesus, but never Jesus alone—only as God the Son with God the Father and God the Spirit, the Three-in-One.

CLARIFICATION 10:
The Old Testament is not "all about" Jesus Christ; even so, the Old Testament is and remains a primary witness to the God that Christians know as Triune: Father, Son, and Holy Spirit.

QUESTIONS FOR DISCUSSION

1. Have you ever thought that the Old Testament's significance lay primarily in how it points to Jesus and the New Testament? Why or why not?
2. Do you find it threatening or uncomfortable to think that the Old Testament does not point to Jesus and the New Testament—at least not primarily? Why or why not?
3. Have you ever read Genesis 3:15 as somehow relating to Jesus? Upon further reflection do you think that is a good reading of the text and in what way(s)?
4. Do you find the Trinitarian approach advocated in this chapter more helpful than a Christological (or Christocentric) one? Why or why not?
5. Identify some other passages (beyond Gen. 3:15) that talk about God that might also, when read with Trinitarian eyes, be seen as referring to Christ and the Spirit. How does this "further reading" help you think about the meaning of Scripture?

CONCLUSION

THE TRUTH ABOUT SCRIPTURE *MATTERS*

James Loewen wrote his best-selling book *Lies My Teacher Told Me: Everything Your American History Textbook Got Wrong* because, in his words, "history can be a weapon" and because false history is "a national problem."[1] Loewen reports that, after working on his book and the many years of speaking, teaching, and writing that followed its publication, he arrived at two additional conclusions. The first is that "the truth can set us free"—an idea that comes, ultimately, from the Bible (John 8:32). The second is that "there is a reciprocal relationship between truth about the past and justice in the present."[2] He ends the preface to his revised edition (published in 2018) with his belief that "most Americans, once they understand why things are as they are, will work to foster justice where there was unfairness and truth where lies prevailed."[3] One worries about that, these days. But hope springs eternal!

It's not hard to apply Loewen's remarks about the study of history to the study of the Old Testament and the attempt I have made in this book to correct some of the many mistruths that we've been taught to believe about it. The truth about the Old Testament, no less than American history (more in fact), can set us free—free to understand Scripture, God, and God's ways in Scripture better than we otherwise do when we operate with misinformation, mistruths, and lies. And Loewen's "reciprocal relationship" between past truth and present justice applies just as well to the Old Testament and contemporary Christian faith and practice as it does to the United States. Among many examples that might be mentioned is this rather disturbing and pressing one: Christian history both early and late shows the perilously close relationship between neglect and denigration of the Old Testament and terrible acts of anti-Semitism. In this connection, we must not miss—but, instead, should closely, even painstakingly examine—how white supremacist groups are often profoundly religious and use the Bible to support their brands of violent racism, which often include anti-Semitism. Such groups don't use the *whole* Bible—of course not! They don't use the whole Bible because the whole Bible is the one that can set them and all the rest of us free—with that "all" including everyone who isn't white too! No, instead, supremacist groups use only a thinned down, censored, selected pastiche of just some verses that, as a result, do not tell the truth, the whole truth, and nothing but the truth—and certainly not *God's truth* as revealed in the entirety of Christian Scripture. Instead, these groups' ideological cherry-picking supports only misinformation, mistruths, and lies. The Holocaust in twentieth-century Europe and the history of slavery and racism, and their continued legacies in North America (and beyond) for the past four hundred years are only the most obvious examples of how mistruths—mistruths *about the Bible*, let the record show—often reap the worst harvests imaginable.

In this connection it is fascinating, to note, per Loewen, that educators "first required American history as a high school subject as part of a nationalistic flag-waving campaign around 1900." And yet, Loewen goes on to write, the "nationalistic genesis" of teaching history "has always interfered with its basic mission: to prepare students to do their jobs *as Americans*."[4] That is because, according to him, by telling lies and half-truths, history teachers and their textbooks have short-circuited the hard work of reading and evaluating the sources and making the hard decisions about the facts that democracies depend on and that democracies require of their citizenry. Half-truths, misinformation, and lies are not hallmarks of democracy, after all, but are instead the insidious instruments used by totalitarian regimes. What we need, therefore, according to Loewen, is

> to produce Americans . . . who command the power of history—the ability to use one's understanding of the past to inspire and legitimize one's actions in the present. Then the past will seriously inform Americans as individuals and as a nation, instead of serving as a source of weary clichés.[5]

So also, we might reason analogically, and with very little difficulty, with reference to the Bible (which is much more, and far less, than "history"), to individual Christians, and to the church. What we need, therefore (to crib once more from Loewen), is

> to produce Christians . . . who command the power of Scripture—the ability to use Scripture to inspire and legitimize our actions in the present. Then Scripture will seriously inform Christians as individuals and as a church, instead of serving as a source of weary clichés.

Weary or otherwise, clichés are easy. So are mistruths: they simplify matters, whether by ignorance, concealment, or duplicity—but they simply will not do. Biblical "half-truths" do real damage. They do not set us free and they also do not set us free to do justice, let alone to love mercy, and to walk humbly with our God, to quote the great prophet Micah (6:8). Instead, even and perhaps especially when they are well-meaning, mistruths like the ones considered in this book (among the many others that might have been mentioned) actually *interfere* with what should be the church's basic mission: to prepare people to do their jobs *as Christians*. God help us to set the record straight for God's sake—and for the sake of God's world.

NOTES

Preface

1. James W. Loewen, *Lies My Teacher Told Me: Everything Your American History Textbook Got Wrong*, 2nd ed. (New York: The New Press, 2018).
2. Loewen, *Lies My Teacher Told Me*, xxv. In a footnote, he notes that perhaps he should have called his book "Lies 70 Percent of My Teachers Told Me" (364 n. 9).
3. Loewen also points out the tension between his title and subtitle: it isn't always the teachers who get things wrong, it's the literature they depend on—misinformed, unhelpful textbooks. Unfortunately, there is an equal if not greater amount of poor information available on the Bible and in every kind of publishing form one might imagine, especially online, including unpublished forms. If teachers rely solely on poor sources, Loewen points out, then they "are complicit in miseducating their charges" (*Lies My Teacher Told Me*, xxv). In my judgment, the same holds true for preachers and teachers in the church.

Introduction

1. James W. Loewen, *Lies My Teacher Told Me: Everything Your American History Textbook Got Wrong*, 2nd ed. (New York: The New Press, 2018).

2. Ken D. Berry, *Lies My Doctor Told Me: Medical Myths that Can Harm Your Health* (Holiday, TN: Berry Pharmacy, 2017); Cole Brown, *Lies My Pastor Told Me: Confronting 18 Church Clichés with the Gospel*, 3rd ed. (Portland, OR: Cole Brown / Humble Beast Records, 2018).

3. Harry G. Frankfurt, *On Bullshit* (Princeton, NJ: Princeton University Press, 2005). This book is only 67 pages long in a very small-sized format and is well worth reading.

4. Lowen, *Lies My Teacher Told Me*, xviii–xix.

Mistruth 1: The Old Testament Is "Someone Else's Mail"

1. The finalization of the canon of the Old Testament didn't take place until some point *after* the Christian movement was on its way and so the statement made here is slightly anachronistic. Even so, it is quite certain that the books that were eventually canonized were available, popular, and widely regarded as authoritative Scripture *before* the formal finalization that came only later. Of course, there was also other literature that was regarded as authoritative and scriptural that did not make the final cut into the Old and New Testament canons. For more on topics like these, see Lee Martin McDonald, *The Biblical Canon: Its Origin, Transmission, and Authority* (3rd ed.; Peabody, MA: Hendrickson, 2007).

2. A possible exception is 2 Peter 3:16, which may consider Paul's writings to be part of the "scriptures," though the specific term used here might be more generic: "writings."

3. It's important to reiterate that Tom likely learned this mistruth from someone else. He didn't get it from the full witness of the New Testament—that's for sure. But Tom isn't alone. Many people make this mistake and pass it along to others. An egregious example from someone who really ought to know better is Andy Stanley, *Irresistible: Reclaiming the New that Jesus Unleashed for the World* (Grand Rapids: Zondervan, 2018). For a sophisticated but still problematic example, see Paul M. van Buren, "On Reading Someone Else's Mail: The Church and Israel's Scriptures," in *Die Hebräische Bibel und ihre zweifache Nachgeschichte: Festschrift für Rolf Rendtorff zum 65. Geburtstag*

(eds. Erhard Blum, Christian Macholz, and Ekkehard W. Stegemann; Neukirchen-Vluyn: Neukirchener Verlag, 1990), 595–606.

4. I take this language, with slight modification, from Ellen F. Davis, *Wondrous Depth: Preaching the Old Testament* (Louisville, KY: Westminster John Knox Press, 2005), 2, who speaks of the Old Testament "as *an immediate presence* that exercises shaping force in Christian lives—indeed, that serves as a source of salutary pressure on our lives." On page xiv, she speaks of the Old Testament as "an urgent and speaking presence."

Mistruth 2: The Old Testament Is a Boring History Book

1. It is now common in historical reckonings to use BCE ("Before Common Era") and CE ("Common Era") rather than BC and AD. The latter abbreviations designate time "Before Christ" and *Anno Domini* (the year of our Lord, not, as is sometimes imagined, "After [Christ's] Death"). Given this shift in convention, I use BCE and CE in what follows but deem them fully interchangeable with BC and AD. If BCE/CE strikes some readers as somehow less religious, it needs only to be remembered that the shift to the common era is still reckoned exactly as it is in the BC/AD understanding—namely, because of the birth of Jesus.

2. See Ellen F. Davis, *Wondrous Depth: Preaching the Old Testament* (Louisville, KY: Westminster John Knox Press, 2005), xiii.

Mistruth 3: The Old Testament Has Been Rendered Permanently Obsolete

1. See further, for example, my own treatment of the issues in Brent A. Strawn, *The Old Testament Is Dying: A Diagnosis and Recommended Treatment* (Grand Rapids: Baker Academic, 2017).

2. See on this point Christopher R. Seitz, *The Elder Testament: Canon, Theology, Trinity* (Waco, TX: Baylor University Press, 2018).

3. A useful and accessible treatment remains Norbert Lohfink, *The Covenant Never Revoked: Biblical Reflections on Christian-Jewish Dialogue* (New York: Paulist Press, 1981).
4. The last qualification is important since the situation here is not unlike the one described earlier (see note 1 in Mistruth 1), namely that the finalization of the canon of the New Testament didn't take place until some point *after* Marcion. In fact, some scholars think that Marcion's heresy provided the impetus to establish the New Testament canon in more definitive fashion. The qualification, "not like we do, at any rate," is thus necessary to avoid anachronism. Be that as it may, there is much debate about these matters, especially around when, exactly, the New Testament canon was fully stabilized. As was the case in speaking of the Old Testament canon in Mistruth 1, it seems quite certain that the books that were eventually canonized in the New Testament were available, popular, and widely regarded as authoritative Scripture *before* the formal finalization that came only later. Similarly, just as with the Old Testament, there was other literature that was also regarded as authoritative that did not make the final cut into the New Testament canon. For more on topics like these, see Lee Martin McDonald, *The Biblical Canon: Its Origin, Transmission, and Authority*, 3rd ed. (Peabody, MA: Hendrickson, 2007).

Mistruth 4: The Old Testament God Is Mean . . . *Really* Mean

1. Abraham Joshua Heschel, *The Prophets* (New York: Harper Collins, 2001), 358–92.
2. Heschel, *The Prophets*, 365.
3. Walker Percy, *Lost in the Cosmos: The Last Self-Help Book* (New York: Picador, 1983), 187.
4. Heschel, *The Prophets*, 367 and 374, respectively.
5. The passage is found in the Babylonian Talmud, Berakhot 7a. It is discussed in Kimberley C. Patton, *The Religion of the Gods: Ritual, Paradox, and Reflexivity* (Oxford: Oxford University Press, 2009), 272 and 444 n. 96.

6. See again Berakhot 7a. I owe this reference to Patton, *The Religion of the Gods*, 265–73.

Mistruth 5: The Old Testament Is Hyper-Violent

1. Definition per *The Oxford English Dictionary* (cited online); the first attestation of the term dates from 1944.
2. An excellent treatment of this issue can be found in R. W. L. Moberly, *Old Testament Theology: Reading the Hebrew Bible as Christian Scripture* (Grand Rapids: Baker Academic, 2013), 41–74.

Mistruth 6: David Wrote the Psalms (and Other Unhelpful Historical Assertions)

1. Billy Collins, "Introduction to Poetry," in *The Apple that Astonished Paris* (Fayetteville: University of Arkansas Press, 2006 [1988]), 58.
2. Augustine, *Confessions*, 12.14.17, cited in Ellen F. Davis, *Wondrous Depth: Preaching the Old Testament* (Louisville, KY: Westminster John Knox Press, 2005), xi.

Mistruth 7: The Old Testament Isn't Spiritually Enriching

1. See Ellen F. Davis, *Wondrous Depth: Preaching the Old Testament* (Louisville, KY: Westminster John Knox Press, 2005), xiii.
2. This language is from Anne Lamott, *Help, Thanks, Wow: The Three Essential Prayers* (New York: Riverhead, 2012). See further Walter Brueggemann, *Spirituality of the Psalms* (Minneapolis: Fortress Press, 2002).

Mistruth 8: The Old Testament Isn't Practically Relevant

1. Dietrich Bonhoeffer, "Lecture on Contemporizing New Testament Texts," in Dietrich Bonhoeffer, *Theological Education at Finkenwalde: 1935–1937*, trans. Douglas W. Stott; ed. H. Gaylon Barker and Mark S. Brocker, *Dietrich Bonhoeffer Works*, vol. 14 (Minneapolis: Fortress Press, 2013), 413–33.

2. To be clear, for Bonhoeffer, God's address to us in Scripture, especially God's work in Christ, is what makes it contemporary. He is talking about the ultimate subject matter of Scripture, that is; he would not advocate, for example, going back to first-century social norms around clothing or the like.

Mistruth 9: The Old Testament Law Is Nothing but a Burden, Impossible to Keep

1. The discussion of Paul and the Law/law is vast. I wish to only note here that it is not always clear that when Paul speaks of "the law" he is always speaking of the Old Testament Law found in the first five books of the Torah (Pentateuch). Indeed, in some cases, it is quite clear he is not speaking of that Law at all.

Mistruth 10: What Really Matters Is That "Everything Is about Jesus"

1. For stories of Jesus raising the dead *before* this parable in Luke, see 7:11–17 (the widow's son) and 8:40–56 (Jairus' daughter; though Jesus says she isn't dead, only sleeping in v. 52). See also 7:22.
2. See J. J. M. Roberts, "The Old Testament's Contribution to Messianic Expectations," in *The Messiah: Developments in Earliest Judaism and Christianity*, eds. James H. Charlesworth et al. (Minneapolis: Fortress Press, 1992), 39–51.

Conclusion

1. James W. Loewen: *Lies My Teacher Told Me: Everything Your American History Textbook Got Wrong*, 2nd ed. (New York: The New Press, 2018), xix.
2. Loewen, *Lies My Teacher Told Me*, xix.
3. Loewen, *Lies My Teacher Told Me*, xix.
4. Loewen, *Lies My Teacher Told Me*, xxvii.
5. Loewen, *Lies My Teacher Told Me*, 362.

SUGGESTED READING

Brueggemann, Walter. *Spirituality of the Psalms*. Minneapolis: Fortress Press, 2002.

Brueggemann, Walter and Tod Linafelt. *An Introduction to the Old Testament: The Canon and Christian Imagination*. 3rd ed. Louisville, KY: Westminster John Knox Press, 2020.

Davis, Ellen F. *Getting Involved with God: Rediscovering the Old Testament*. Cambridge, MA: Cowley Publications, 2001.

_____. *Wondrous Depths: Preaching the Old Testament*. Louisville, KY: Westminster John Knox Press, 2005.

_____. *Opening Israel's Scriptures*. New York: Oxford University Press, 2019.

Handy, Lowell K. *The Educated Person's Thumbnail Introduction to the Bible*. St. Louis: Chalice Press, 1997.

Lamb, David T. *God Behaving Badly: Is the God of the Old Testament Angry, Sexist, and Racist?* Downers Grove, IL: InterVarsity Press, 2011.

Strawn, Brent A. "And These Three Are One: A Trinitarian Critique of Christological Approaches to the Old Testament." *Perspectives in Religious Studies* 31.2 (2004): 191–210.

_____. *The Old Testament Is Dying: A Diagnosis and Recommended Treatment*. Grand Rapids: Baker Academic, 2017.

_____. *The Old Testament: A Concise Introduction.* New York and London: Routledge, 2020.

Wright, Christopher J. H. *The God I Don't Understand: Reflections on Tough Questions of Faith.* Grand Rapids: Zondervan, 2008.

CPSIA information can be obtained
at www.ICGtesting.com
Printed in the USA
LVHW082025090221
678835LV00014B/2338